CAMBRIDGE LIBRARY COLLECTION

Books of enduring scholarly value

History

The books reissued in this series include accounts of historical events and movements by eye-witnesses and contemporaries, as well as landmark studies that assembled significant source materials or developed new historiographical methods. The series includes work in social, political and military history on a wide range of periods and regions, giving modern scholars ready access to influential publications of the past.

An Inquiry, Whether Crime and Misery Are Produced or Prevented, by Our Present System of Prison Discipline

Thomas Fowell Buxton, M.P. (1786–1845) was a philanthropist who had many connections with the Quaker movement through the family of his wife, who was the sister of Henry Gurney and Elizabeth Fry. He was a passionate opponent of slavery, and campaigned to end it at a time when most British people believed that enough had been done by the abolition of slave trading in 1807. His other great interest was the punishment of crime: he wanted the death sentence abolished, and his campaign succeeded in reducing the number of capital crimes from over two hundred to eight. This book is a plea for a complete change in the purpose and operation of prisons, and an argument (still valid today) that prisons actually encourage crime and produce recidivists rather than reformed characters. Buxton draws on own his experience as a visitor to produce a harrowing account of Victorian prison conditions.

Cambridge University Press has long been a pioneer in the reissuing of out-of-print titles from its own backlist, producing digital reprints of books that are still sought after by scholars and students but could not be reprinted economically using traditional technology. The Cambridge Library Collection extends this activity to a wider range of books which are still of importance to researchers and professionals, either for the source material they contain, or as landmarks in the history of their academic discipline.

Drawing from the world-renowned collections in the Cambridge University Library, and guided by the advice of experts in each subject area, Cambridge University Press is using state-of-the-art scanning machines in its own Printing House to capture the content of each book selected for inclusion. The files are processed to give a consistently clear, crisp image, and the books finished to the high quality standard for which the Press is recognised around the world. The latest print-on-demand technology ensures that the books will remain available indefinitely, and that orders for single or multiple copies can quickly be supplied.

The Cambridge Library Collection will bring back to life books of enduring scholarly value (including out-of-copyright works originally issued by other publishers) across a wide range of disciplines in the humanities and social sciences and in science and technology.

An Inquiry, Whether Crime and Misery Are Produced or Prevented, by Our Present System of Prison Discipline

Thomas Fowell Buxton

CAMBRIDGE UNIVERSITY PRESS

Cambridge, New York, Melbourne, Madrid, Cape Town, Singapore,
São Paolo, Delhi, Dubai, Tokyo

Published in the United States of America by Cambridge University Press, New York

www.cambridge.org
Information on this title: www.cambridge.org/9781108004923

This edition first published 1818
This digitally printed version 2009

ISBN 978-1-108-00492-3 Paperback

AN INQUIRY,

WHETHER

CRIME AND MISERY

ARE

PRODUCED OR PREVENTED, BY OUR PRESENT SYSTEM

OF

Prison Discipline.

ILLUSTRATED BY DESCRIPTIONS OF

THE BOROUGH COMPTER.
TOTHILL FIELDS.
THE JAILS AT ST. ALBANS,
AND AT GUILDFORD.

THE JAIL AT BURY.
THE MAISON DE FORCE AT GHENT.
THE PHILADELPHIA PRISON.
THE PENITENTIARY AT MILLBANK.
AND THE PROCEEDINGS OF THE LADIES' COMMITTEE AT NEWGATE.

By THOMAS FOWELL BUXTON.

"I make no scruple to affirm, that if it were the aim and wish of Magistrates to effect the destruction, present and future, of young delinquents, they could not desire a more effectual method than to confine them in our Prisons."—HOWARD.

"Whereas, if many offenders convicted of crimes, for which transportation has been usually inflicted, were ordered for solitary confinement, accompanied by well-regulated labour and religious instruction, it might be the means, under Providence, not only of deterring others from the commission of the like Crimes, but also of reforming the individuals, and inuring them to habits of Industry, &c."—19 GEORGE III. c. 74. s. 5.

London:

PRINTED FOR JOHN AND ARTHUR ARCH, CORNHILL; BUTTERWORTH AND SONS, FLEET STREET; AND JOHN HATCHARD, PICCADILLY.

1818.

PREFACE.

BEING at Ghent during the early part of this winter, I took some pains in examining the excellent prison of that city, known by the name of the Maison de Force. On my return to England, I communicated to the "Society for the Improvement of Prison Discipline, and for the reformation of juvenile offenders," the intelligence which was thus acquired. The members of that institution had accurately investigated the state of almost every jail in the metropolis and its vicinity. Their inquiries had led them to a decided and unanimous conviction, that the present alarming increase of crime arose more from the want of instruction, classification, regular employment, and inspection *in Jails,* than from any other cause, and that its prevention could only be accomplished, by an entire change in the system of prison discipline. These views were strongly confirmed by the practical illustration afforded by the Maison de Force, and this led to a request from the Committee, that the description of it might be published.

When I sat down to this task, the work insensibly grew upon my hands. It was necessary, to prove that evils and grievances did really exist in this country, and to bring home to these causes, the increase of corruption and depravity. For this purpose repeated visits to various prisons were requisite.

Again a detail of the regulations of the Maison de Force alone, did not seem to establish the point contended for, with sufficient certainty. An experiment might succeed abroad, which might fail at home. Local circumstances and the habits of the people, might have rendered a plan very judicious in the Netherlands, which was quite impracticable in England. It appeared therefore desirable, to shew, that whether the attempt be made on the Continent, in England, or in America, the same results are invariably displayed.

This occasioned a new series of inquiries.

While I was occupied in procuring this intelligence, which was intended to be printed at a distant period, the unexpected appointment of a Parliamentary Committee to examine the jails of this city, and the discussions which took place in the Court of Common Council, attracted much attention to the point. It was probable that this session would not pass, without some legislative enactment upon the subject. If the intended communications were of any importance, the time seemed arrived for making them. The immediate publication of even crude and undigested materials was better calculated to do good to the cause, than a more finished and elaborate treatise, when general interest may have subsided.

The haste with which the parts of this Pamphlet were put together, in the last fortnight, and the consequent impossibility of any revision, must explain, if they do not excuse, many obvious errors in expression, and numerous inaccuracies in printing. For the truth of the facts, no indulgence is required. Every method has been used to discover their authenticity. Nothing is stated, (with the exception of the account of the Philadelphia Jail) which has not come within my own observation, and which has not been confirmed by the concurrent testimony of the gentlemen, who have been my companions. The descriptions of the Borough Compter, Tothill Fields, the Penitentiary, the Jails at St. Albans, at Bury, and at Ghent, have been read to their respective jailers, and that of Guildford was handed to a magistrate of the County of Surrey, with a request that he would point out any mistakes.

I have generally mentioned the days on which I visited jails, the persons with whom I went, and, where I could do it with propriety, the names of any prisoners whose case attracted my particular attention. I have done this as inviting inquiry, as placing my statements in a more tangible shape, and as furnishing a facility for the detection of errors.

Feeling no uneasiness as to the accuracy of the facts related, I must confess I have felt some repugnance to the disclosure of scenes, which may be considered as reflecting discredit on those who ought to have prevented them; but against the pain which this pamphlet may give to the affluent and the powerful, must be weighed, the secret sufferings, the unknown grievances, the decay of health, and corruption of morals, which by its suppression, may be continued to the inmates of many dungeons in this country. I have great confidence in the power of public opinion, in preventing detected wrong; and if this confidence be not misplaced, all option upon my part ceases, the publication becomes a matter of imperative duty; to conceal would be to participate.

I will conclude this Preface by stating, that none of the grievances represented, are occasioned by the jailers; that class of men are often subjected to undistinguishing abuse, my experience would furnish me with very different language. Without any exception, I have had reason to approve, and sometimes to applaud their conduct; and I can truly say, that of all the persons, with whom I have conversed, they are the most sensible of the evils of our present system of prison discipline.

AN

INQUIRY,

&c.

Magna Charta declares that no freeman shall be taken or imprisoned, but by *the lawful judgment of his equals*, or the *law of the land.*

When a prisoner is convicted by the "lawful judgment of his equals," imprisonment is sometimes a part, and sometimes the whole of the penalty awarded against him; and evidently with the strictest justice, because it is proved that he has been guilty of an offence, and this is the appointed punishment.

But the "law of the land" finds it necessary to depart from this rigid rule of equity, which would abridge only that man of his freedom, who had been pronounced a delinquent by the verdict of his peers. The security of the whole demands, that the liberty of some should be suspended for a certain period. Persons are accused of crimes—they may be innocent, or they may be guilty: but their detention is necessary until the time arrives in which one or the other can be established; yet, they are innocent in the eye of the law, till their guilt is proved; and in this case imprisonment is not imposed as a penalty, it is merely permitted as the only method of insuring the appearance of the person suspected, on the day of trial.

So far does the law carry its reluctance to impose confinement before conviction, that it allows the accused, where the imputed offence is not of an heinous description, to be at large on giving bail for his appearance; * it does not do so in cases of greater enormity, because the man who has committed a capital offence, and therefore anticipates the loss of his life, as well as of his property, will not be deterred from making his escape by any securities he may have given. The ancient law displayed even still more tenderness towards the liberty of the subject, for " by it, in all cases of felony, if the party accused could find sufficient securities, he was not to be committed to prison, *quia carcer est mala Mansio.* † It soon appears however, that one exception was allowed to this rule, Glanvil ‡ says, in all charges of felony the accused is admitted to bail, except for the death of a man, where, for terror's sake, it is otherwise determined. The law, says Lord Coke on Magna Charta, favouring the liberty and freedom of a man from imprisonment (though it were for the most odious cause, the death of a man) and that he should not be detained in prison until the Justices in eyre should come, provides that he might sue out a writ of inquisition directed to

* Commitment for trial being only for safe custody; wheresoever bail will answer the same intention, it ought to be taken. Book iv. chap. 22. *Blackstone.*

† Coke 2 Inst. chap. xv. p. 185. note 5.

‡ Lib. xiv. chap. 1.

the Sheriff; * and the 3rd of Edward the 1st, chap. 15, after pointing out by many and careful restrictions the cases in which alone bail can be refused,—declares if any withhold prisoners replevisable after they have offered sufficient security, he shall pay a grievous amerceament to the King."

In short, to use the expressive words of Lord Coke, "the Law did highly hate the long imprisonment of any man" before trial:

Now it is not to be believed that our ancestors, feeling so much solicitude for the conservation of the freedom of the untried, were unconcerned about their state, when the public welfare demanded their confinement. It is as evident by the law of the land, as it is by plain reason and the palpable rules of justice, that the man whom it is found expedient to confine, should be treated with the utmost possible lenity,—that suffering some degree of necessary hardship by the privation of his liberty before trial; that privation should be rendered as mild and as little galling as possible, by every reasonable indulgence compatible with his safe custody. All beyond this, every act which produces needless restriction or suffering, is an act of wrong and of oppression.—Laws may be as severe against crime as were the laws of Draco, with some colour of justice: Mistaken legislators may imagine that this merciless system may alarm mankind into innocence; but no principle of justice can defend the infliction of any severities on the unconvicted. A man can avoid

* Coke on Magna Charta, chap. 26.

the penalties of crime, by avoiding all criminality; but no man is secure against false accusation; and to condemn him who is only suspected, to any thing beyond mere confinement, is to commence his punishment when his crime is uncertain.

Lord Coke says, with his usual quaintness, "The philosophical poet doth notably describe the damnable and damned proceedings of the judge of Hell.—

> Gnossius hic Rhadamanthus habet durissima regna,
> Castigatque, auditque dolos.—

"First he punisheth, and then he heareth; but good judges and justices abhor these courses."*

There is another description of persons who are deprived of their liberty by the law of the land, namely, those in debt.—The debtor may have been guilty of improvidence, of desperate speculations, or of fraudulent wastefulness; but he may have been reduced to his inability to satisfy his creditor by the visitation of God,—by disease, by personal accidents, by the failure of reasonable projects, by the largeness or the helplessness of his family. His substance and the substance of his creditor, may have perished together in the flames, or in the waters. Human foresight cannot always avert, and human industry cannot always repair the calamities to which our nature is subjected;—surely these are entitled to some compassion. The Committee of Aldermen appointed to visit various prisons, are of a different opinion: they think, "that on no consideration ought indulgence to be carried so far in a prison, as that it shall cease to punish as a prison;" and

* 2nd Inst. c. 29, on Magna Charta.

they give this reason :—"we should fee. that we wanted compassion for the industrious and injured creditors of this city, many of whom earn their daily bread by labour, from the rising to the setting sun; were we so far to contemplate the situation of these debtors, as to place them within the walls of a prison with greater comparative comforts than the families of the citizens, whom they have not only wronged, but upon whom by their habits of idleness and dissipation, they have, in many instances, entailed absolute ruin; and who have been induced by their specious appearances and artful means, to improvidently trust them."

Surely it cannot have escaped these gentlemen, that this very paragraph confutes their presumption, that prisoners for debt are always fraudulent; because it produces an instance in which insolvency is not a fraud. Let us follow their own picture of a citizen :—He earns his daily bread by labour, from the rising to the setting sun; he is imposed upon by the specious appearances and artful means of the idle and the dissipated; he is unable to discharge the demands against him, and a jail is his fate. Thus, the very man for whom so much tenderness is expressed, may become their victim.—To punish him, by a sweeping declaration that prisons ought always to punish, is to scourge misfortune with those rigors which guilt alone can deserve.

The law of the land, however, appoints imprisonment for debt; and it is not my present purpose to inquire, whether in this instance that law is too rigorous; but that it is not too lenient, is evident by universal confession, and by the various contradictory, and often unjust expedients to which the legislature has resorted, to abate the severity of its own enactments.

Imprisonment is then the legal consequence of debt: but it is only imprisonment, and it must not be accompanied with unnecessary and often fatal concomitants. Not an act in the statute book is to be found, which by any mode of construction can be distorted into a justification of any, even the slightest severity upon the debtor, beyond his imprisonment. With respect then to the untried debtors, confinement is adjudged by law; but whatever goes beyond mere confinement, whatever has a tendency to impart moral or physical evil, to disgust or to irritate their feelings, is injustice;—and injustice the more dreadful, because it is inflicted on a class of men who are already too often weighed down by misfortune—because it is inflicted in places where the public eye does not penetrate, where therefore, public compassion is not excited; but whether it be more or less dreadful, is not so much the question. This, I conceive, is certain, that any unnecessary severity to the prisoner who has not been tried, or the prisoner for debt, is injustice.

I am ready to admit, that the hardship of loading the convicted delinquent with rigors which are not required for his safe custody, is less evident. On the first view of the subject, we are apt to imagine that this is a part of his punishment; but it is not so in the contemplation of the law.—That law ascertains the nature, and in some cases the Judge determines the quantum of the punishment, according to the aggravations of the crimes; but the penalty thus pronounced, is all that is to be inflicted: where the law, therefore, condemns a man simply to be committed to jail, the suspension of his personal liberty is the utmost which he ought to suffer; and to embitter his confinement by circumstances often much worse than the loss of liberty itself, is to aggravate and distort the law, and to annex severities which are not awarded by its sentence. I am well aware that the law itself, in certain cases, renders imprisonment more rigorous by express provisions:— In cases of murder, "the offender shall be fed with bread and water only, and confined in a cell apart from the other prisoners;" but this peculiar severity appointed in certain cases, implies that it is not to be exercised in others where no such appointment is made.

It is therefore evident, I conceive, that where the law condemns a man to jail, and is silent as to his treatment there, it intends merely that he should be amerced of his freedom, *not that he should be subjected to any useless severities.* This is the whole of his sentence, and ought therefore to be the whole of his suffering.

If any one should be disposed to hesitate in the adoption of this opinion, and should still cling to the idea, that prisons ought to be, not merely places of restraint, but of restraint coupled with deep and intense misery; let him consider the injustice, and irresistible difficulties which would result from such a system. If misery is to be inflicted at all in prisons, it ought surely to be inflicted with some proportion to the crime of the offender; for no one could desire to visit very different degrees of guilt with the same measure of punishment. Now this is utterly impracticable. Our prisons are so constructed, as in many instances to prevent the possibility of any separation at all, even between the tried and the untried, the criminal and the debtor, the insane, the sick, and the healthy. If it be difficult to separate those amongst whom the difference is so broad and palpable, how would it be possible to relax or to aggravate imprisonment according to the varying circumstances of each case? There must be as many distinctions as crimes, and almost as many yards as prisoners. And who is to apportion this variety of wretchedness? The Judge who knows nothing of the interior of the jail, or the jailer who knows nothing of the transactions of the Court? The law can easily suit its penalties to the circumstances of the case. It can adjudge to one offender imprisonment for one day; to another, for twenty years; but what ingenuity would be sufficient to devise, and what discretion could be trusted to inflict modes of imprisonment with similar variations?

In fact, prisons must always, certainly under our present modes of policy they must, contain masses of offenders, with very different shades and distinctions of guilt; and we must either make imprisonment as bitter as possible, and thus involve the comparatively innocent, in those hardships which we impose upon delinquency of the deepest hue, confounding all notions of equity; or we must come to the conclusion that imprisonment is nothing more than privation of liberty, and ought therefore to be attended with as little of what is vexatious, and as little of what is hurtful as possible. Let no one apprehend that he is called upon to embrace any new opinion; the doctrine is older than the statute book—it existed, when the existence of the House of Commons is a matter of conjecture. Bracton says, that fetters and all such things are forbidden by law; because a prison is a place of retention, and not of punishment, lib. iii. folio 105. Fleta says, l. i. c. 26, jailers shall not increase the punishment of those committed to their care, nor shall they torture them; but all severity being avoided, and all mercy being exercised, they shall duly execute their sentences. Lord Coke says, all the said ancient authors are against any pain or torture being inflicted upon a prisoner before attainder; nor after the attainder, but according to the judgment.

Taking along with us the principle which has here been stated, we must next consider particularly the treatment which a prisoner should receive; and the equitable principle seems to be, that he should suffer no damage either in mind or body, which is not found in his sentence; that his situation should not be worse than it was before his commitment, with the single exception of the loss of liberty. This can only be done by general rules. You cannot exactly adapt his treatment in prison to his preceding circumstances; but by the establishment of equitable and liberal regulations, you may guard against any violent infraction of justice; and if you err at all it will be on the side on which we should all wish to err—the side of humanity.

Let us then follow a prisoner from his first commitment, always remembering that as yet his guilt is unproved. You have no right to march him along the streets in chains, or to make him a spectacle of public ignominy, perhaps on the very spot, and amongst the very people with whom he has hitherto held a fair character.—Infamy may be the penalty for crime, but it should never be the consequence of suspicion: you should, therefore, conduct him to his jail with every possible attention to his feelings; with decency and secrecy. When he is entered within its walls, you have no right to load him with irons; you have no right to subject him to bodily pain from their weight, or to that agony of mind, which must result from such symbols of degradation to a man of yet unblunted feelings; and you have no right to conclude that he is not such. And here I must observe in the language of Blackstone,* "The law will not justify jailers in fettering a prisoner, unless where he is unruly, or has attempted an escape." It would be tedious to the generality of my readers to confirm so high an opinion by additional authorities: it is sufficient to say that such are to be found in the Myrror,† in Coke,‡ and in Bracton; the latter, indeed, goes so far§ as to intimate, that a sentence condemning a man to be confined in irons, is illegal.

* Book iv. c. 22. † C. 5. § 1—54. ‡ Ins. 3—34. § L. 3—105.

Lord Chief Justice King replied to those who urged that irons were necessary for safe custody, "that they might build their walls higher." The neglect of this legal precaution is no excuse for the infliction of an illegal punishment: nor will it, I presume, be contended, that when Magistrates neglect their duty, prisoners should suffer for it. The truth is, a man is very rarely ironed for his own misdeeds, but very frequently for those of others: additional irons on his person, are cheaper than additional elevation to the walls.—Thus we cover our own negligence, by increased severity to our captives.

You have no right to abridge him of pure air, wholesome and sufficient food, and opportunities of exercise. You have no right to debar him from the craft on which his family depends, if it can be exercised in prison. You have no right to subject him to suffering from cold, by want of bed-clothing by night, or firing by day; and the reason is plain,—you have torn him from his home, and have deprived him of the means of providing himself with the necessaries or comforts of life, and therefore you are bound to furnish him with moderate, indeed, but suitable accommodation.

You have for the same reason no right to ruin his habits, by compelling him to be idle; his morals, by compelling him to mix with a promiscuous assemblage of hardened and convicted criminals; or his health, by forcing him at night into a damp unventilated cell, with such crowds of companions, as very speedily to render the air foul and putrid; or to make him sleep in close contact with the victims of contagious and loathsome disease, or amidst the noxious effluvia of dirt and corruption. In short, attention to his feelings mental and bodily, a supply of every necessary, abstraction from evil society, the conservation of his health and industrious habits, are the clear, evident, undeniable rights of an unconvicted prisoner.

He should be brought to his trial as speedily as possible, for every hour of unnecessary delay in furnishing him with the opportunity of proving his innocence, is, at least may be, an hour of unjust imprisonment.

At his trial, either he is acquitted,—in which case the least you can do, is to replace him in the situation you found him, to pay his expenses home, and to furnish him with sufficient to support him till he has had an opportunity of looking out for work: or he is convicted,—and then it is for the law to appoint the punishment which is to follow his offence. That punishment must be inflicted, but you must carefully guard that it be not aggravated, and that circumstances of severity are not found in his treatment, which are not found in his sentence. Now no Judge ever condemned a man to be half starved with cold by day, or half suffocated with heat by night; who ever heard of a criminal being sentenced to catch the Rheumatism or the Typhus Fever? Corruption of morals and contamination of mind, are not the remedies which the law in its wisdom has thought proper to adopt. We should remember, to use the words of a former writer on the subject, "that disease, cold, famine, nakedness, a contagious and polluted air, are not lawful punishments in the hands of the civil magistrate; nor has he a right to poison or starve his fellow-creature, though the greatest of criminals."*

The convicted delinquent then has his rights.—All measures and practices in prison, which may injure him in any way, are illegal, because they are not specified in his sentence:—he is, therefore, entitled to an wholesome atmosphere, decent clothing and bedding, and a diet sufficient to support him.

But besides the rights of the individual, there are duties to the community:—*Parum est improbos coercere pœnâ, nisi probos efficias disciplinâ.*—One of the most important of these duties is, that you should not send forth the man committed to your tuition, in any respect a worse man, a less industrious, or a less sober, or a less competent man than when he entered your walls. Good policy requires that, if possible, you should dismiss him improved.

For the improvement of the unconvicted prisoner, you should labour, as a recompense for his confinement before trial—that thus you may convert the suspicion of crime into its prevention in future—that thus you may addict him to such habits, and instil such principles, and impart such instruction as may repair the damage you have done him; and that he, being amerced of one period of his life, may be enabled to spend the remainder more respectably.

* State of Jails, by W. Smith, 1776.

For the improvement of the debtor you should labour, because the grand causes of debt are sickness, idleness, or intemperance:—you must therefore, provide against its recurrence by those measures which may secure the health, the industry, and the sobriety of your prisoners. The convicted criminal is also entitled to your care. Our law *is not*, in its true spirit, whatever it may be in its modern execution, a system of bloody vengeance; it does not say, so much evil is repaired by so much misery inflicted. A merciful and enlightened jurisprudence, like the Author of all that is merciful and wise, does not rejoice in the death of a sinner; but rather, that he should turn from his wickedness, and live. Punishments are inflicted, that crime may be prevented, and crime is prevented by the reformation of the criminal. This may be accomplished. The prisoner being separated from his former associates, ceases to think as they think: he has time for recollection and repentance, and seclusion will humble the most haughty, and reform the most abandoned.

It is then necessary that he sleep alone, and that he be alone during a great portion of the day.

But as idleness is one great cause of sin, industry is one great means of reformation. Measures must, therefore, be taken for his constant employment, and for making that employment agreeable by allowing him to share largely in its profits.

The use of stimulating liquors is often the cause, and always the concomitant of crime. These, therefore, must be forbidden. The want of education is found to be a great source of crime; for this, therefore, a provision must be made. The neglect of religious duties is the grand cause of crime. Ministers of religion must, therefore, be induced to give their active and zealous labours to the prisoners daily, reading prayers in public, and giving private instruction. The assiduous services of such men will not be fruitless. Mr. Robinson of Leicester declared that no part of his ministry had been so signally blessed as that in the jails; and the Ladies' Committee of Newgate have many proofs that reformation may be accomplished, even amongst the most dissolute and abandoned.

Such then, as I have described, being the rights of all prisoners, and such our policy, I maintain that these rights are violated, and this policy is abandoned, in England. The prisoner, after his commitment is made out, is handcuffed to a file of perhaps a dozen wretched persons in a similar situation, and marched through the streets, sometimes a considerable distance, followed by a crowd of impudent and insulting boys; exposed to the gaze and to the stare of every passenger: the moment he enters prison, irons are hammered on to him; then he is cast into the midst of a compound of all that is disgusting and depraved. At night he is locked up in a narrow cell, with, perhaps, half a dozen of the worst thieves in London, or as many vagrants, whose rags are alive, and in actual motion with vermin: he may find himself in bed, and in bodily contact, between a robber and a murderer; or between a man with a foul disease on one side, and one with an infectious disorder on the other. He may spend his days deprived of free air and wholesome exercise. He may be prohibited from following the handicraft on which the subsistence of his family depends. He may be half starved for want of food and clothing, and fuel. He may be compelled to mingle with the vilest of mankind, and in self-defence, to adopt their habits, their language, and their sentiments; he may become a villain by actual compulsion. His health must be impaired, and may be ruined, by filth and contagion; and as for his morals, purity itself could not continue pure, if exposed for any length of time to the society with which he must associate.

His trial may be long protracted; he may be imprisoned on suspicion; and pine in jail while his family is starving out of it, without any opportunity of removing that suspicion, and this for a whole year:—if acquitted, he may be dismissed from jail without a shilling in his pocket, and without the mean of returning home:—if convicted, beyond the sentence awarded by the law, he may be exposed to the most intolerable hardships, and these may amount to no less than the destruction of his life now, and his soul for ever. And in the violation of his rights, you equally abandon your own interest. He is instructed in no useful branch of employment, by which he may earn an honest livelihood by honest labour. You have forbidden him to repent and to reflect, by withholding from him every opportunity of reflection and repentance. Seclusion from the world has been only a closer intercourse with its very worst miscreants; his mind has laid waste and barren for every weed to take root: he is habituated to idleness, and reconciled to filth, and familiarized with crime. You give him leisure, and for the employment of that leisure you give him tutors in every branch of iniquity. You have taken no pious pains to turn him from the error of his ways, and to save his soul alive. You have not cherished the latent seeds of virtue, you have not profited by the opportunity of awakening remorse for his past misconduct. His Saviour's awful name becomes, indeed, familiar to his lips, because he learns to use it, to give zest to his conversation, and vigor to his execrations; but all that Saviour's office, his tenderness, and compassion, and mercy to the returning sinner, are topics of which he learns no more, than the beasts which perish. In short, by the greatest possible degree of misery, you produce the greatest possible degree of wickedness; you convert, perhaps, an act of indiscretion into a settled taste, and propensity to vice. Receiving him because he is too bad for society, you return him to the world impaired in health, debased in intellect, and corrupted in principles.

The object of this book is to prove the existence of these facts, and that their continuation is as unnecessary as it is detrimental, to the best interest of society; in fact, that cruelty to your prisoner, is impolicy to yourself. I am well aware that an awful responsibility rests upon the man who makes such heavy charges. He must prove them by evidence clear and undeniable, by facts strong and sufficient in themselves, precise in their application, and beyond all question as to their accuracy; or he must be content with the appellation of a libeller: if they be true, they merit the attention of the public, and the interference of the legislature; if false, there is no term of reproach which may not justly be cast upon the Inventor of such slander.

With these warning considerations pressing upon my mind, *and prepared for this alternative,* I proceed to the proof.

The Borough Compter.*

Our prisoners have all that prisoners ought to have:—without Gentlemen think they ought to be indulged with Turkey carpets.

Parliamentary Debates.

THIS prison belongs to the city of London, and its jurisdiction extends over five parishes.—On entrance, you come to the male felons' ward and yard, in which are both the tried and the untried—those in chains and those without them—boys and men, —persons for petty offences, and for the most atrocious felonies; for simple assault, for being disorderly, for small thefts, for issuing bad notes, for

* Visited:—December 16th, 1817—and January 26th, 1818—January 30th—February 3d; with S. Hoare, jun. Esq. Banker; and I have his authority to say, that his observations concur in every respect with my statements. Feb. 16th—*when I read this description to the Governor, which he confirmed in every particular.*

forgery and for robbery. They were employed in some kind of gaming, and they said they had nothing else to do. A respectable looking man, a smith, who had never been in prison before, told me that "the conversation always going on, was sufficient to corrupt any body, that he had learned things there, that he never dreamed of before."

You next enter a yard nineteen feet square; this is the only airing place for male debtors and vagrants, female debtors, prostitutes, misdemeanants and criminals, and for their children and friends. There have been as many as thirty women; we saw thirty-eight debtors, and Mr. Law, the Governor, stated, when he was examined, that there might be about twenty children.*

On my first visit, the debtors were all collected together up stairs. This was their day-room, bed-room, workshop, kitchen, and chapel. On my second visit, they spent the day and the night in the room below; at the third, both the room above, and that below were filled. The length of each of these rooms, exclusive of a recess, in which were tables and the fire-place, is twenty feet. Its breadth is three feet, six inches for a passage, and six feet for the bed. In this space twenty feet long, and six wide, on eight straw beds, with sixteen rugs, and a piece of timber for a bolster, twenty prisoners had slept side by side the preceding night: I maintained that it was physically impossible; but the prisoners explained away the difficulty by saying, "they slept

* Report of the Committee of the House of Commons.

edgeways." Amongst these twenty, was one in a very deplorable condition; he had been taken from a sick bed, and brought there; he had his mattress to himself, for none would share it; and indeed my senses convinced me that sleeping near him, must be sufficiently offensive.

I was struck with the appearance of one man, who seemed much dejected; he had seen better times, and was distressed to be placed in such a situation. He said he had slept next to the wall, and was literally unable to move, from the pressure. In the morning, the stench and heat were so oppressive, that he and every one else on waking, rushed, unclothed as they must be, into the yard; and the turnkey told me, that "the smell on the first opening of the door, was enough to turn the stomach of a horse."

I cannot reflect on the scene I witnessed without grief; almost every man looked ill, and almost every one who had been here any time, said he had had a severe illness; we were all immediately struck with their squalid appearance. It may perhaps be supposed, that we were duped by our imaginations; that observing the closeness, and want of exercise to which they were subjected, and ascribing to these causes their usual effect, we concluded without sufficient examination, that the prisoners must be unhealthy. The following fact, for the accuracy of which, I appeal to my respectable companions,* will evince that I describe not

* Mrs. Fry, St. Mildred's Court; Miss Sanderson, Old Jewry; members of the Ladies' Committee of Newgate;—Mr. Crawford, Se-

merely what I expected to see, but what we actually saw. I called my friends together, and requested their attention: I then addressed myself to one of the prisoners at another part of the room, to whom we had not previously spoken, and said, "I perceive by your appearance, you have not been here long?"—"Only nine days," was his answer. To another, "I fear you have been here some time?" "Yes, Sir, three months." To another, "You have been here very long, I should suppose?"—"Nearly nine months." In fact, I pointed out five, and from their looks predicted nearly the period of their confinement, nor was I once deceived.

I have seen many hospitals and infirmaries, but never one to the best of my belief, in which the patients exhibited so much ill health. The following facts deserve attention: on my second visit there were thirteen persons confined on criminal charges, of whom five were under the Surgeon's hands, as cases of Typhus Fever. On my first visit we observed in one of the cells, a lad in bed, and seemingly very ill with Typhus Fever; the window was closed, and the reason given was, that the air would be dangerous to him; yet the preceding night two

cretary of the society for the prevention of juvenile delinquency.—Mr. Wood, an active member of the Philadelphia Society for prisoners; the latter Gentleman subsequently told me, that, shocked as he had been at the general state of our prisons, nothing had struck him so deeply as the deplorable wretchedness manifest in the countenances of these prisoners.

other prisoners had slept with him in a room seven feet by nine. The three were,

JAMES M'INTOSH, charged	with felony.
THOMAS WILLIAMS, ...	with stealing a piece of gingham.
JEREMIAH NOBLE, ...	with an assault.

And no alteration was intended, neither indeed was any possible.

We conceived that to place others, for the night, in this corrupt and infected air, close by the source of that infection, was inevitably to taint them with disease. This conjecture was unhappily verified; for at my next coming, I observed in the list of those who had been seized with fever, the names of Thomas Williams, and Jeremiah Noble.* Now, mark the case of Jeremiah Noble; he is charged with an assault, and the law condemns him to a short imprisonment, preparatory to his trial. But the regulations of the city inflict on him, in addition, a disease very dangerous in its nature, very suffering in its progress, and very enfeebling in its consequences. The vigor of his constitution may surmount it, but all prisoners have not vigorous consti-

* The following minutes are extracted from the Surgeon's book:

Dec. 10.—M'Intosh has a feverish complaint.

Dec. 14.—M'Intosh better, the other prisoners healthy.

Dec. 27.—Williams, Noble, and Rawlins, are ill.

Dec. 30.—The above are attacked with fever.

Observ.—M'Intosh is declared to be ill of a fever on the 10th, and on the 16th, I find that Williams and Noble had slept with him the preceding night.

tutions: thus the most venial offence, which calls down the visitation of the law,* a debt of one shilling, or a fraud to the amount of one penny,† may be punished with a lingering and painful death.

Now, it is evident, that the regulations of this prison are calculated to produce disease, and to communicate it: The next question is, what measures are taken to cure it? Till very lately there was no Surgeon or Apothecary provided, nor any medicine allowed. At this moment there is no in-

* What is the smallest debt for which you have ever known a prisoner in that prison? *Ans.* I have known them there for one shilling.—*Evidence of Mr. Law, keeper of the Borough Compter, before the Police Committee,* 1814.

† Some friends of mine, who are indefatigable in visiting prisons, saw in a yard at Coldbath Fields, four men and thirty boys; amongst the rest, a lad of fifteen years of age, whose open countenance induced them to enquire into his case. He was employed by a Corn Chandler, at Islington, and sent by his master with a cart and horse to London. There is in the middle of the City Road, a temporary bar, at which I have sometimes seen a collector of tolls, and sometimes not.

He passed through this without paying the toll of one penny, declaring he saw no person there: he was summoned before a magistrate the next day, fined forty shillings, and in default of payment, sentenced to a month's imprisonment. My friends inquired into the character of his parents, and found them highly respectable. The father, the present, and the former master, gave the boy a very good character; and the latter, a small shop-keeper, offered ten shillings towards his release: by the payment of the fine he was happily released. Had he passed a month with the associates with whom he was placed, it will hereafter appear that it is more than possible he would have been ruined for ever. Upon his discharge, he thanked the gentlemen in the most grateful terms; adding, I will always be a good boy, and never get into prison again.

firmary. When a debtor is ill, he is separated from the others by a blanket; but how effectual that separation must be which takes place in a room of 20 feet in length, in which 20 persons sleep side by side, will require no peculiar sagacity to determine. When a criminal is ill, however infectious may be his complaint, however offensive, however requiring quiet, there is generally no separation at all. I observed in the Surgeon's book, a multitude of judicious observations as to the unwholesomeness of the prison, amongst the rest the following:

October 7, 1817.

"The prison is clean, but from its crowded state there are seven requiring medical assistance;—if fever ensue in consequence, the greatest danger is to be apprehended from a total want of accommodation to separate the sick."

(Signed.) W. H. Box.

I fear I shall hardly be credited when I assure my readers, that as yet, I have not touched upon that point in this prison which I consider the most lamentable; the proximity between the male debtors and the female prisoners. Their doors are about seven feet asunder, on the same floor; these are open in the day time, and the men are forbidden to go into the women's ward;—but after the turnkey left us, they confessed that they constantly went in and out; and there is no punishment for doing so.*

* In the hot nights of summer, when the prison is very full, the

That this is the fact, appears by the evidence of the Governor before the Police Committee. *Ques.** Is it possible for the men to get into the sleeping wards of the women? *Ans.* I cannot say that it is impossible. Is any thing done to prevent them, if the parties consent? No.

Thus the male debtors reside, (without any partition but an open space of seven feet), close by females sent there for debt, for assaults, for misdemeanors, and for prostitution. Am I not warranted in saying, that the regulations of this prison encourage licentiousness? For what is to prevent promiscuous intercourse, and public acts of obscenity, except the directions of the jailer at a distance, or the virtue of those females who are imprisoned for the want of it. Females are sometimes accused of offences, of which they afterwards demonstrate their innocence. Maid servants, in respectable families, of hitherto unblemished reputation, may be, and are, often charged in error, with purloining small articles belonging to their master or mistress. Imagine an innocent girl, who had hitherto been shielded from even allusions to vice, brought to this prison, and placed at once within the view and within the range of this unbridled harlotry. Can her mind escape pollution? Can she shut her eyes and her ears to the scenes which are passing around her? Is not residence in this place, (however innocent she may

Governor has to choose between the evils of excluding the air by shutting the doors, or admitting the men, by opening them; that is—between disease and dissoluteness.

* Committee on State of Jails, in London, 1814, page 61.

have been of the imputed crime), an eternal stain upon her character? The law is justly jealous of female reputation; but here, as if forgetful of its own principles, it robs the unprotected, and often innocent girl of her fair name, exposes her virtue to temptation, and places before her eyes, vice in its worst and most degrading realities. To answer to all this, that those who come here, cannot be made worse, is to say, that female debtors are always prostitutes, and that accusation is proof. I can well conceive that where prisoners are guilty of some petty offence alleged against them, yet that they may not be utterly depraved; a girl for the gratification of her vanity, may secrete an article of dress: she is very wrong, but because she has descended one step in the scale of vice, it does not follow inevitably, that she has fallen to its lowest abominations. But it may be said I overstate the case; that the opening of the doors is an event of rare occurrence; and that the rules of the prison, (to the violation of which no penalty is attached,—in fact, therefore, the recommendations of the jailer) may have weight enough to stifle the calls of licentious passion. Be it so.—There is at least one scene of gross and revolting indelicacy which no female can escape. There is but one yard and one privy for men and women, and every woman must pass through this yard. The turnkey on the one hand, and the more respectable of the debtors on the other, told me that it was always an occasion for coarse jests, and "for a piece of fun."

I pass over some other points without comment;

such, for instance, as the window of the room of the female debtors and misdemeanants, being so near to the felons' yard, as to allow of conversation, which, as the Governor told me, often occasions the most offensive language; so offensive, indeed, that the debtors had lately complained of it; but I would seriously address myself to those who have the power to alter these enormities.

In the courts of Aldermen and Common-council, the majority are men of property, education, and feeling. I would ask each amongst them, who has a daughter, whether he would not rather follow her to her grave, than see her placed in such a dreadful brothel. And while the subject is before them, and before Parliament, I will fairly declare my opinion, that if invention had been racked to discover methods of corrupting female virtue, nothing more ingeniously effectual could have been discovered, than the practices of the Borough Compter. Perhaps that attention may be paid to the recommendations of a visiting magistrate, which may be withheld from an unauthorized individual as I am. I extracted the following observations from the minute book:—

"I am compelled to lament the utter impossibility of classification, to prevent the union of persons charged with all offences; and, moreover, to notice the great impropriety of female felons being introduced in the day, not only to female, but to male, debtors; having but one yard for the joint recreation, and necessary purposes."

(Signed) JAMES WILLIAMS.
July 22, 1817.

The date of this observation is very remarkable. It is the last which appears in the visiting magistrates' book. Thus, this prison, within less than five minutes walk of London Bridge;—a prison which outrages every feeling of common humanity, which is really shocking, and melancholy, and disgraceful; —a prison, in which the period of each man's captivity may be judged by the degree of languor and sickliness visible in his countenance;—a prison, the regulations of which openly violate the law of the land, and are the direct reverse of the rules recommended by the Committee of Aldermen;*—a prison, in which I have witnessed as much of what is truly deplorable and dismal, as it ever was my misfortune to behold; in which it is difficult to determine, whether the vice it encourages is, or is not, surpassed by the measure of misery it inflicts. This prison has not, as far as it appears, been visited by one single official person, capable of redressing the slightest of its atrocious evils, for a period of more than six months.

No cooking utensils are provided. The allowance of food is fourteen ounces of bread per day, and one pound of the "clods and stickings of beef" twice per week. I maintain that this is a system of starvation.

Let the magistrates especially, who appoint this as a sufficiency of diet—let any person—compare this quantum of food with their own consumption, and he will need little authority to induce him to

* Report, p. 5. Printed, 1815.

concur with me; but I will mention the information I received from a lady, who must know the realities of the case, and who is above all suspicion of exaggeration. A person very competent to judge, told me, "that those who have only the prison-allowance gradually decline in health. Four women and four children have lately died in Newgate, whose death may be ascribed, in great part, to the want of food."

No provision of labour is appointed. At my first visit to the debtors, by the kindness of the jailer,* some were employed in making shoes and clothes, and expressed their gratitude, for the ease to their minds, and the relief to their families, which this labour afforded; one, the father of a large family, was engaged in repairing his *children's* shoes. But when I next went, the crowded state of the prison rendered work impossible. As I stood in the yard, instead of hearing as I have elsewhere heard, the sounds so grateful in a prison, the rap of the hammer, and the vibrations of the shuttle, our ears were assailed with loud laughter, and the most fearful curses; when we entered, we saw three separate parties at cards, one man reading a novel, and one sitting in a corner intent upon his Bible.

No soap is allowed; there is no school; and a prisoner, when he arrives, is turned in amongst the rest without any examination as to the state of his

* Mr. Law is a man of great humanity, which he has evinced, as I know, by many efforts to procure situations for discharged prisoners, as well as by every possible attention to the cleanliness and comfort of those who are committed to his care.

health. This may account for a remark in the apothecary's book, January 5th, 1818.—"Some of the prisoners have contracted the itch." The case of one man struck me much: he was found in a most pitiable state in the streets, and apprehended as a vagrant; he was at first placed with the debtors, but he was so filthy and so covered with vermin, (to use the expression of the turnkey, "he was so lousy,") that his removal was solicited. I saw him lying on a straw-bed, as I believed at the point of death, without a shirt, inconceivably dirty, so weak as to be almost unable to articulate, and so offensive as to render remaining a minute with him quite intolerable; close by his side, four other untried prisoners had slept the preceding night, inhaling the stench from this mass of putrefaction, hearing his groans, breathing the steam from his corrupted lungs, and covered with myriads of lice from his rags of clothing; of these, his wretched companions, three were subsequently pronounced by the verdict of a jury "not guilty," and of these one was Noble, whose case I have before described. The day after their discharge, I found the two who were convicted almost undressed: on asking the reason, they said their clothes were under the pump to get rid of the vermin received from the vagrant; his bed had been burnt by order of the jailer; his clothes had been cut off, and the turnkey said, one of his companions had brought him his garter, on which he counted upwards of forty lice.

The jailer told me "that in an experience of nine years he had never known an instance of reformation; he thought the prisoners grew worse, and that he was sure, that if you took the first boy you met with in the streets, and placed him in his prison, by the end of a month, he would be as bad as the rest, and up to all the roguery of London;" half his present prisoners have been there before, and upon an average he thinks if one hundred are let out, he shall soon have twenty to thirty back again, besides those who go to other jails.

I will not trouble my reader with any further observations upon this prison, but he must determine for himself, whether crime and misery are produced or prevented in the Borough Compter.

Tothill Fields.*

The first yard you enter is for felons, tried and untried, boys and men; at the end of this is an open iron railing, within is the narrow airing place of the infirmary; beyond is the vagrants' court, equally connected with the infirmary by open iron work. Thus the patients communicate with the vagrants on one side, and the felons on the other; nothing surely could be more admirably contrived for the interchange of physical and moral contagion.

Many of the wards, in which the prisoners sleep, are sunk below the level of the ground, and this level is considered to be below high water mark. The up-stairs rooms of the Governor's house are much affected with damp; hearing this from himself, I could not suspect the truth of the statements of the prisoners, who complained bitterly of the cold and moisture of these cells. To obviate these inconveniences, as many as possible crowd together at night into the same cell;—how injurious this must be to health, can be conceived by the statement of

* Visited:—December 26, 1817; and February —, 1818; with S. Hoare, jun. Esq. and Mr. Crawford; and on February 20, 1818, I read this statement to the jailer, requesting him to point out any error: he confirmed every particular.

the jailer, who told me that having occasion lately to open one of the doors in the night, the effluvia was almost intolerable. My readers will naturally ask—what is the result of these *precautions against health?* I will answer by facts. We saw a woman lying in one of the wards, who seemed very ill. The apothecary happened to come in at this moment; upon examining her, he said to the keeper—"she is ill just like the rest." We asked what is her complaint?—Acute rheumatism.—What is the cause?—The dampness.—Is it a common complaint here?—Yes.—Elsewhere?—No.—Out of every hundred, how many here, upon an average, are seized with acute rheumatism?—About ten.*—Are you surprised at the largeness of the proportion?—Not at all, I often wonder it is not larger.—How many pass through this prison in a year?—About two thousand. Is it possible, that a complaint not easily removed by all the remedies which opulence can procure, and very painful in its attacks, is thus annually inflicted, (to take the lowest computation) on upwards of one hundred persons. In the infirmary I saw a veteran sailor, who had landed troops at the battle of Bunker's Hill, and had fought with Nelson at the battle of Trafalgar; he had, he said, never had an hour's illness till he came here.

Straw, and a blanket for two men, is the allowance of bedding.

* Truth obliges me to confess, that when I repeated this question to the Governor, he did not think the number could fairly be estimated at above six in every hundred.

Debtors, in this prison, are entitled to much commiseration. The rule is:—

For a debt under 20*s*.— 20 days' confinement.

——————— 40*s*.— 40 days' confinement.

Thus persons may be, and *have been* sent here for 20 days, for a debt of 2*s*. 6*d*., and no provision is appointed for them. They are not legitimately entitled to one ounce of bread. It is presumed they do not want it. It is presumed that those who are confessedly unable to ransom themselves from this destructive dungeon, by a petty payment, are competent to support themselves while within it. One would have thought that the man who comes here, gives a sufficient demonstration of his poverty; but, as if it were a conclusive proof of his riches, it is presumed, without any investigation, that no allowance to him is necessary; if he be, (what ninety-nine out of every hundred, who are arrested for debts, under twenty shillings are) a pauper, he must depend upon charity—or he must draw his subsistence from his family, who, already distressed, are rendered utterly destitute by the suspension of his labour—or he must starve; or the jailer, by a charitable violation of rule, must grant him provisions. Surely the humanity and fairness of these presumptions, ought to be re-considered, especially when it is recollected that a Coroner's inquest in October last, on the body of John Burden, declared, that he died for want of proper nourishment.

St. Albans.

WE first went to the Borough Jail,* which is *a wooden building*.

A girl was confined in the day-room, the window at which she sits, opens to the street, with which it is nearly on a level. We, standing in the street, conversed with her, and the bars are wide enough to admit any thing, of which the bulk is not very considerable; of course spirits could not be excluded. On the Sessions day, this window is closed by a shutter, as it was found that the prisoners got drunk, and were in that state during their trial. The jailer opened a door, of what appeared to us a dark closet, assuring us that when we entered we should be able to see;—and, in fact, we could discover the dimensions by the light admitted through the crevices of a hole,

* Visited January 29, 1818, with S. Hoare, Jun. Esq. I first sent these statements to the Sheriff of the County, requesting him to examine their accuracy, but he returned them to me, stating, he had no jurisdiction in St. Albans. I then sent them to a gentleman who resides there, and for whose kindness to the prisoners I had heard much gratitude expressed, begging him to read it to the jailers, and to examine whether I had fallen into any mistake. He pointed out two small errors, which I have corrected; and adds, "every thing else is exactly as you have described."

which had been formerly stopped up, at the top of the room. To this day-room for men, (in which the difference between night and day is hardly discernible) the only entrance was through the women's apartment.

The bed-rooms were equally incommodious. The men and women are separated by an open railing, the bars of which are about *six inches* distant from each other, and the only air, or light, admitted to the men's apartment, is through this lattice. The allowance of food is one pound and a half of bread per day, and no firing is provided, in fact it would be needless, for there is no fire-place. It is to be observed, there is no yard. How far the exposure at all times, by this open intercourse with the male prisoners at night, and with all persons in the street in the day, may improve the morals and delicacy of the females; and how far the seclusion from all air, and light, and exercise, may affect the health of the men, experience alone can determine.

To restrict the prisoners to one pound and a half of bread; to exclude the males from light, and the females from the possibility of retirement; to deny them fire on the one hand, and exercise on the other, are violations of natural justice; and in my estimation, and, I think, in the estimation of all impartial men, are neglects most serious in their nature, and far more destructive in their consequences, than those crimes which are punished with so much rigor.

It must, however, be observed, that the culprits committed here are very few in number.

Abbey of St. Albans' Gateway, Jan. 20, 1818. *House of Correction on one side, and Jail for the Liberty of St. Albans, on the other; separate establishments.*

House of Correction, generally for Persons sentenced to hard Labour.—There is no salary for a clergyman, and no provision of labour: as for correction, therefore, these prisoners are left to improve themselves; with no other assistance than the conversation and examples of their associates. One pound and a-half of bread is the daily allowance to each individual, and no firing. The room in which they pass the day, cook their victuals, and sleep at night, was very close, and emitted a very offensive smell. The necessary is in a closet in the same room. The bed consisted of straw on the floor, with four blankets and two rugs, for five men; one of them looked exceedingly ill. There is no infirmary, no clothes are allowed, and all were very ragged. I asked the jailer, Do you think the prisoners' morals improve by coming here? "No, Sir, quite the contrary, they do one another mischief; they go out worse than they come in, and so it must be, till old offenders are separated from the others, and till they are employed."

The Jail for the Liberty of St. Albans.—No fire; one pound and a-half of bread per day. I asked the jailer if this was sufficient? Some, he said, could eat double as much. No separation, except between men and women. The men's sleeping-room is without air or light, except what may be received through a grating, which opens into a passage, which opens into the day-room, which communicates with the yard. The building is an old fortification, and into this room there is one of the loop-holes, which are common in such buildings; but this was stopped to exclude the cold air. When the door was open, it was so dark, that we hesitated about entering, being unable to perceive whether there was or was not a step. We were informed there was a load of straw, which we never saw: one blanket and some straw is the bedding allowed. The men are employed in making straw hats, baskets, &c. A manufacture of straw has been introduced by the kindness of a neighbouring gentleman, and the prisoners expressed their pleasure in having the employment, as it filled up their time, and they earned something: all had learnt this except one cripple. Women have no work at all. In the absence of the keeper, we asked the men to tell us truly, whether they were worse or better for being there. A decent looking man answered,—in truth, Sir, we all grow worse,—I confess I have.

I asked the jailer the same question; his answer was—"If I must say the truth, they do all grow worse; they go out more corrupted than they come in; it must be so. There are in that yard all manner of offenders. That boy," mentioning a lad of about 20, "robbed his master in London, and was committed to Newgate, and condemned to be hanged. He was saved by the intercession of his father, who is a very respectable and opulent man; he robbed his father to a great extent, and he is sent here for eighteen months for another robbery. Now he is such a desperate wicked character, as to be sufficient to corrupt all the boys, and men too, that come here in that time; he knows all the practices of London, and has told them to his companions. In the same yard are several boys for poaching, for keeping sporting dogs, and slight offences."

"Have you," I asked, "ever known persons come here comparatively innocent, who have gone out quite depraved?" "I have not known persons come here innocent, because they are sent here for some offence; but I have known several sent here for first offences, whose minds were not wicked, though they had been guilty of the one offence. I have known a great many, (I can't mention the number) who, coming in thus, have gone out quite depraved; but I never knew one who, coming in wicked, went out better."—"How," I asked, "could you endeavour to improve them, if you had sufficient accommodation?" "Why that is a question that requires a good deal of consideration; I can't at once say all I would do, but certainly I would—

"1. Separate the tried from untried.

"2. Boys from men; those for great crimes and those for lesser offences: in short, I would separate them as much as possible, for the more there are, the worse they are.

"3. I would employ them all; for when they are employed, they are not plotting mischief, nor telling stories, nor quarrelling, nor fighting."

He added—"Solitary confinement always produces the effect I want."

I am persuaded, that if every jailer of England were examined they would subscribe to this opinion. The clergyman of the Borough, Mr. Small, is very attentive, and officiates without salary.

On going out, we observed some girls before the windows, and the male prisoners amusing themselves in spitting at them.

Guildford.*

This is the school, in which so many brave men have been made.—
Beggars' Opera.

In this jail the prisoners complained much of cold, and not unreasonably, as I thought, for the day-room for all of them, at this time amounting to thirty-five, and at one period of the year for a short time amounting to as many as one hundred, is nine

* February 4th, with S. Hoare, jun. Esq. Before I left the prison, I read each memorandum to the jailer, for the purpose of ensuring accuracy, and subsequently sent this statement to a magistrate of the county, whom I knew to be interested in the subject, requesting him to point out any mistakes.

feet ten inches by nine feet six inches; eight feet three inches high. It is therefore evidently impossible, in snow, or rain, or frost, for them to obtain shelter or warmth. A prisoner, however, has the privilege, if he requires it, of being shut up all day in his sleeping cell, with unclosed windows and without fire, and these cells are opened in very severe weather.

There is no Infirmary, and no possibility of separating the healthy from the sick. They must sleep together, and the rooms must be crowded. Low fever was very prevalent in the autumn; there were as many as six cases at a time: had the disorder been very contagious, the consequences, in the Governor's opinion, must have been dreadful.

There is no chapel, service in fine weather is performed in the yard, in the winter it is often dispensed with.

There is no work, several prisoners from the country complained of this, and said they were so tired of doing nothing, that they should be happy to work, if they received no part of the earnings: in this opinion however the prisoners sent from London did not seem to concur.

There is no classification: a man charged with murder, several convicted of housebreaking, one for bastardy, and some deserters, had lately occupied one cell. Amongst the commitments, we observed vagrants, poachers, persons charged with assaults, a man for getting drunk in a workhouse, refractory farming servants; and these must herd during the day and the night with most hardened criminals.

There is no privy; The consequence of all this is, that the prisoners are dirty to an extreme, are very abject and sallow in their appearance, have generally had severe colds and rheumatism; and, if the Governor is to be credited, leave prison worse in every respect than they entered it. Forty-five years experience has not furnished him with an instance of an individual reformed by imprisonment; but innumerable instances of petty offenders converted into proficients in crime, several of this kind he detailed to me. Many years ago, a lad of the name of John Haines, was sent from the country, charged with an assault; in prison he formed a connection with a female, with whom he afterwards lived: he became one of the most noted highwaymen that ever infested the neighbourhood of London, and was executed.

Two boys were lately committed for poaching; they appeared at first quite strangers to crime, and kept themselves at a distance from the other prisoners. Their reserve, however, soon left them; they listened with eagerness to the adventures and escapes of their associates; they determined to go to London, and the day after their term of imprisonment was expired, they called at the jail to receive the promised letters of introduction from the thieves in prison, to their companions and receivers in town. Happily the Governor had observed the progress of their depravation, had received an intimation that they were to be furnished with these credentials, and very properly refused them admittance. The bedding is straw, with a blanket and a rug between two persons.

No prison dress is allowed, and nearly half were without shirts, or shoes or stockings. The moment a prisoner arrives, he is turned in among the rest, however filthy or diseased he may be.

The irons are remarkably heavy—and all who are confined for felony, whether for re-examination, for trial, or convicted, are loaded with them; and those who are double ironed cannot take off their small-clothes. The food is one pound and a half of the best bread and nothing else, the jailer said that many of them had friends, who sent them provisions—and these did very well; but many who had been apprehended at a distance, never received any thing beyond the Prison allowance, and in such cases he observed a gradual decay of health.

Let it never be forgotten, that of these poor creatures, some are vagrants; often Irish labourers, who have fled from starvation at home, and wandered into England in search of employment, guilty of begging to sustain life; some are convicted of the most trifling offences, and many are untried; that is, after having spent a night wedged in with this mass of uncleanness, they may be proved, on the morrow, as innocent of the imputed crime as the Judge who tries them.

Is this justice,—is it humanity? We live in a free country, and we boast that the rights of the meanest man amongst us, are as inviolable as those of the greatest; we are followers of Christianity, which teaches that we should do unto others as we would that others should do unto us; but we must renounce our pretensions to the one, and abdicate the principles of the other, or we must correct these high and grievous abuses.

I asked the Governor his opinion of the jail; he said it had only one good point: the two largest cells were so strong, no prisoner could break out of them.

There is however, another excellent circumstance; the windows of his rooms look directly into the yard, consequently he can observe all that passes: he frankly confessed that this was his only real security, "for the eye of the jailer would do more than locks, or walls." His observation upon the moral influence of the prison, is that old thieves from London, corrupt boys from the country; and that they make it a system to teach each other all the wickedness they know. After they have once been in, they soon return, or he hears of them from London; and if all his prisoners were released that day, he should expect two-thirds of them back again in six months. We then asked him what would be his plan if he could build a jail, and appoint regulations at his own discretion. He said,

First, They should all have separate cells of a night; two should never sleep together.

Secondly, They should be much separated by day, and classed according to their degrees of crime.

Thirdly, They should all be employed, and hard at work; regular thieves would hate this, and labouring men would be more likely to take to work when they got out.

It is easy enough to repeat the observation of the

jailer, and to state the accommodations of the prison, but I feel that I have much failed in doing justice to the appearance of the prisoners. Misery was displayed more evidently in their dress, and written in more legible characters on their countenances, than in any jail I ever entered.

It is a matter of great satisfaction to me, to be able to state, that the magistrates of Surrey are not insensible of the condition of this and their other prisons; and have come to a determination to erect establishments, suitable for the confinement, separation, employment, and reformation of their prisoners.

HAVING thus entered into a detail of prisons—in London, in Middlesex, in Hertfordshire, and in Surrey. I abstain from exhausting the patience of my reader by any further local description of this kind;—because I have the presumption to think that nothing more is necessary to establish the accuracy of each charge which I have made against our present system of prison discipline. Let no one, however, conclude, that those prisons in the vicinity of London, which are not mentioned, are free from every possible imputation. I could dispense with the Borough Compter, Tothill-fields, St. Albans, and Guildford; and yet establish my case beyond all contradiction. There are undoubtedly gradations in the inhumanity which is practised towards prisoners, and in (I may say) the *exertions* which are used to corrupt them; yet the same principle reigns very generally throughout. This will be best illustrated by a few facts: at the House of Correction at Chelmsford,* I was advised by the jailer not to enter, as sickness was very prevalent: it appeared that one youth had died in the morning, of the small-pox,

* Visited, Jan. 6, 1818.

and one was (as it was supposed) dying of the Typhus Fever. The County jail at Kingston,* is, in most respects, a counterpart of that of Guildford: the same want of work, clothing, cleanliness, and classification; and the same report from the jailer, of the encreasing depravity of the prisoners. The town jail is a public house,* in the tap-room of which, the debtors were sitting, in the center of a crowd of other visitors.

At Horsemonger Lane House of Correction,† the cells are about six feet by eight, sometimes as many as five, and constantly three are placed within them for the night. We measured the bedstead, it is twenty-two inches wide; when three sleep together, one must lie on the floor, and the other two are accommodated by lying on the bed in opposite directions, the feet of the one in contact with the face of the other.

In Coldbath-fields‡ we saw in a yard of which there is no inspection, and in a retired cell in that yard, three men and a boy. The men had been tried, convicted, and sentenced, for attempts at the most disgraceful and most abominable of crimes. The boy, a lad of seventeen years of age, of very decent appearance, committed by a magistrate on the complaint of his master, for idleness.

Many and very grievous are the instances which have come to my knowledge of persons corrupted

* Visited in company with Mr. S. Hoare, Feb. 4, 1818.

† Visited with Mr. S. Hoare in January, 1818.

‡ Visited with the Honourable H. G. Bennett, Jan. 17, 1818.

by prison. When I first went to Newgate, my attention was directed, by my companion, Mr. Bedford, of Stewart Street, Spitalfields, to a boy whose apparent innocence and artlessness, had attracted his notice. The schoolmaster said he was an example to all the rest, so quiet, so reserved, and so unwilling to have any intercourse with his dissolute companions. At his trial, he was acquitted, upon evidence which did not leave a shadow of suspicion upon him: but lately I recognised him again in Newgate, but with a very different character. I cannot entertain a doubt of this lad having been ruined by Newgate. I could, if delicacy would allow it, mention the name of a person who practised in the law, and who was connected by marriage with some very respectable families. He, for a fraud, was committed to Clerkenwell prison, and sent from thence to Newgate, in a coach, handcuffed to a noted housebreaker, who was afterwards cast for death. The first night, and the subsequent fortnight, he slept in the same bed with a highwayman on one side, and a man charged with murder on the other. During that period, and long after, spirits were freely introduced. At first he abstained from them, but he soon found that either he must adopt the manners of his companions, or his life would be in danger. They already viewed him with some suspicion, as one of whom they knew nothing. He was in consequence put out of the protection of their internal law. Their code is a subject of some curiosity. When any prisoner commits an offence against the community, or against an individual, he is tried. Some one, generally the oldest and most dexterous thief, is appointed judge; a towel tied in knots is hung on each side of his head, in imitation of a wig. He takes his seat, if he can find one, with all form and decorum; and to call him any thing but "my lord," is a high misdemeanour. A jury is then appointed, and regularly *sworn*, and the culprit is brought up. Unhappily justice is not administered with quite the same integrity within the prison as without it. The most trifling bribe to the judge will secure an acquittal, but the neglect of this formality is a sure prelude to condemnation. The punishments are various, standing in the pillory is the heaviest. The criminal's head is placed between the legs of a chair, and his arms stretched out are attached to it, he then carries about this machine; but any punishment, however heinous the offence, might be commuted into a fine, to be spent in gin, for the use of the Judge and Jury. This mode of trial was the source of continual persecution to Mr. ——, hardly a day passed without an accusation against him for moving something which ought not to be touched, or leaving a door open, or coughing maliciously, to the disturbance of his companions. The evidence was always clear, to the satisfaction of the Jury; and the Judge was incessant in his efforts to reform him, by inflicting the highest punishments. In short, self-preservation rendered it necessary for him to adopt the manners of his associates; by insensible degrees he began to lose his repugnance to their society; caught their flash terms, and sung their songs, was admitted to their revels, and acquired, in place of habits of perfect sobriety, a taste for spirits; and a taste so strong and so rooted, that even now he finds it difficult to resist the cravings of his diseased thirst for stimulants.

I conceive I cannot better illustrate the situation of Mr. ——, than by a letter I received from his wife. Considerable suspicion must attach to the declaration of every person, however reputable his present conduct may be, who has been himself convicted of crime: I have, therefore, thought it right to suppress every part of his information which is not confirmed by other and creditable testimony. The artless statement of his wife, who has throughout conducted herself with unimpeachable propriety, and who laboured with her own hands to support her husband when in confinement, will hardly be rejected.

"Sir,

"I cannot attempt to state to you the sufferings I have undergone, from the first period of my husband's persecution, to his final release. Passing over my having to attend him for near a month at the Clerkenwell prison, previous to his removal to Newgate for trial; where, on my first visit to him, I found he had been so removed, handcuffed to a notorious offender; now become an inmate in the same ward with several others of the most dreadful sort, whose language and manners, whose female associates of the most abandoned description, and the scenes consequent with such lost wretches, prevented me from going inside but seldom, and I used to communicate with him through the bars from the passage; but on my going one morning, I found he was ill, and unable to come down. Anxious to see him, I went to the ward, and there he lay, pale as death, very ill, and in a dreadful dirty state, the wretches making game of him, and enjoying my distress; and I learned he had been up with the others the whole night. Though they could not force him to gamble, he was compelled to drink; and I was afterwards obliged to let him have eight shillings to pay his share, otherwise he would have been stripped of his clothes. I was the more shocked, as knowing Mr. ——'s firm mind and sober habits, up to this moment. I dreaded the consequences of such a relaxation and of such examples. I saw his health declining; I saw the destructive effects upon him of such association; I found he was compelled to do as they did, and to think as they thought; for on his once attempting to remonstrate with them, his life was threatened, and he was afraid when he went to bed to go to sleep. Having this relation from him, and seeing him daily getting worse; knowing his former strict principles and steady habits, I felt every thing a wife could feel for a virtuous man and an affectionate husband, forced into such society; and his irretrievable ruin, even in this respect, presented itself to my view."

It is remarked by Mr. Locke—" Of all the men we meet with, nine parts in ten are what they are, good or evil, useful or not, by their education." Let us pause for a moment, and consider what education we bestow upon those whom we place under the tuition of a jailer. It is an observation which every man who marks what passes before his eyes must have made, that the human mind arrives at enormity in guilt by a slow and gradual advance.

Nemo repente fuit turpissimus.

Vice is a monster of such hideous mien,
As to be hated needs but to be seen;
Yet seen too oft, familiar with her face,
We first endure, then pity, then embrace—

are the results of ancient and modern experience.

Let us suppose, then, a youth in the commencement of his career of crime; so far guilty as to have incurred the milder visitations of the law, but yet not entirely lost to a sense of virtue, and the possibilities of reformation. Let us imagine him placed in precisely the same predicament as those youths, whose unhappy story I have traced in the description of the Borough Compter; spending his days with the vicious, and his nights with the diseased; receiving from the first, that instruction which may fit him for the perpetration of crime, and imbibing from the second, the seeds of that debility which will unfit him for every thing else. In this state of mind and body, at the expiration of his term of confinement, you throw him at once upon the town without a shilling in his pocket, his next meal depending upon the dexterous application of those lessons of fraud which have been his only recent acquirement. He must starve, or he must rob ; you have taken from him the means of honest labour, but you have initiated him into other and more gainful arts. He came to your prison a misdemeanant ; you send him from its walls a criminal—wasted in strength, polluted in principles, and ruined in character. All respectable men reject him, because they know that to have been in your prison, is to be corrupted. He is compelled by the cravings of nature, to take refuge amongst the hordes of thieves ; they receive him with open arms, supply his immediate necessities, and advance him money on account, to be repaid by the product of his future depredations. They laugh away his scruples, if the society in which you had placed him had left him any, and soon furnish him with an opportunity of displaying his gratitude, his courage, and his proficiency. His is then a rapid career, he soon knows every haunt of vice, and is known by the fraternity of thieves as a willing labourer in any branch of their calling ; his face grows familiar to the officers of justice ; he has soon passed through half the prisons in the metropolis ; till at length he stands at the bar, convicted of some act of desperate enormity ; the dreadful sentence of the law is passed upon him, and all hopes of mercy are forbidden. The judge, the magistrates, the jury, the spectators, are shocked at such an instance of youthful depravity, while their hearts whisper, " Thank God, I am not as this robber." But if he who sows the seed contributes to the production of the harvest, they may find other subjects of astonishment than his guilt, *and accomplices where they least expect them.* Let them look to the cause, and they will discover in this monster of crime, a wretched, pitiable victim, of the careless indifference of the public. I do not hesitate to say, his blood is upon us all; upon the magistrates, who do not provide suitable places of confinement; upon us, the public at large, for if we did but feel a lively desire to avert and to prevent these terrible scenes of villany and vice; if a general feeling were excited and loudly expressed throughout the country, our prisons might be made schools of reformation.

Let no one imagine, that the representation I have here given of the progress of crime is a fanciful picture, which is seldom, if ever, realised. There is a society in this city for the prevention of juvenile delinquency. By the most assiduous labours, by continual visits to boys in prison, and by offering a ready ear to their distresses when out of it; by giving advice to some, small sums of money to others, procuring situations for those of whom they entertained strong hopes of reformation; by restoring some to their friends, sending some to the country; by taking some as servants into their own families: in short, by every method which active and discreet benevolence could devise, they have procured a fund of information and of evidence, which puts the above statement beyond all dispute. Amongst other records, they have a bulky lexicon of all the slang terms in use: I mention it as a curiosity. But they have also a document of great importance—a catalogue of the names, residence, and age of several hundred juvenile depredators; the company they keep, the places to which they resort, and, in many instances, a history of their progress in vice, from their first deviation from virtue. They have seen many cases of boys, who, upon their first coming to prison have kept at a distance from the other prisoners, and appeared grieved and shocked at their situation and companions; by the next visit this bashfulness had fled, they were mingled amongst the men or the boys; at the next, all difference between them and the oldest offenders had vanished, they had learnt the language, were fluent in the oaths, and doubtless had caught the spirit of their associates. Soon after their exit from jail, these gentlemen generally receive tidings, that such a boy had been very clever, meaning that he had been very successful. Before long, they recognize him in some other prison, and hear from the turnkey that he is a most desperate and wicked character. He may hereafter escape the rigour of the law, by his dexterity; he may rise to the command and the captaincy of an associated number of youthful robbers; avoiding personal danger, he may direct their operations, and divide their plunder. On the other hand, he may not obtain promotion; his genius may be too humble to elevate him above the ranks; he may be, as some have been, in prison 28 times; he may be sent to the Hulks, or transported to Botany Bay. Whatever be his outward state, within he is irretrievably ruined. To say that such is the usual consequence of confinement according to our present system, is to say only what is warranted by experience; but a single instance will perhaps illustrate its truth, more than any general declaration. In the case which I am about to produce, I have examined every particular with the most minute attention, and have such evidence of its accuracy, as would be admitted as incontestable in a court of law.

T. M.* now residing in the neighbourhood of Moorfields, was a butcher, in comfortable circumstances, at Barnet. By personal enquiry, I found that he had been much respected there by his neighbours, and was considered a man of probity. He engaged in farming at the time when the price of corn and meat opened very flattering prospects; but the depression which subsequently took place, reduced him to insolvency. He now is a journeyman butcher in London, and his master gives him the highest character; and some gentlemen in his neighbourhood, merely on the score of his good behaviour, have employed him and his wife to clean their school.

His son G. M. was educated at the endowed Grammar School at Barnet, under the Rev. Mr. Marr, who writes me word, "G. M. was for some time under my care, and, as far as I recollect, conducted himself properly during that period." He came to London with his father; and I am assured,

* I have thought it prudent to suppress the name, because the reformation of the boy is within possibility; but if any gentleman is desirous of examining the accuracy of the statement, I will furnish him with the address of the father, who has read this statement, and is ready to corroborate every part of it.

by a very respectable tradesman, who knew him well, that he would not have objected to take him into his service. He is now fourteen years old, and a boy of an intelligent countenance. He was apprehended in May last, as a vagrant, for selling religious tracts, in Bishopsgate Church Yard, without a Hawker's License, and committed to the City Bridewell for a month. There he passed the day with twenty men and four boys committed for various crimes: and he slept with an Irishman who employed him to pick pockets and steal from the other prisoners, and received, as the boy says, the produce of his thefts. The man and five others took a fever, and the boy continued to sleep with him during its progress. He caught it himself, brought it home, and communicated it to his father, mother, and three brothers, of whom one died. His nurse and her family were seized with it, and have not recovered at this moment. On his return, he was so covered with vermin, that his parents were obliged to destroy the blankets and rug of his bed. The father told me, that before his apprehension, he was a good and dutiful son, and that he had no fault to find with him: his mother said he was a quiet demure boy, fond of reading, and always willing to go with her to a place of worship. Now he never takes a book into his hands, except to purloin it; and if she mentions any religious service, she is answered by execrations on her and her advice. She placed him in the school in Angel Alley, but he sent word to the master, with a desperate oath, that he would never go again. She cannot keep any work in the house: he has stolen and sold her Bible, his father's clothes, and the clothes lent by the Raven Row School to his brother: he is seldom at home: his father has found him at night sleeping in the baskets of Covent Garden, with a horde of girls and boys,—thieves and prostitutes. I was much struck with the behaviour and feeling lamentations of his parents. They spoke to the boy " more in sorrow than in anger," and even excused his unkindness and depravity as resulting from this confinement. On the other hand, I was as much struck with the hard, careless, scornful manner in which he replied.

One cannot think upon the conduct of this boy without feelings of the deepest reprobation; but let us turn from his crimes to his misfortunes, and perhaps we shall find that depraved as he is, " he is more sinned against than sinning." I think the charge of corrupting him is clearly brought home to our system of prison discipline. Had he been separated from others: had he been kept to regular employment, there is every reason to think that he would have remained innocent: if he offended against the law of the land in a slight degree, that law, at least the present practice, offended most grievously against him—for in addition to the award of the court, he has lost his character, his principles, and every hope of future respectability. Against the parents—for they have lost the affections and duty of one child, and the life of another: against the welfare of society—for it has added to the number of its foes, for it has debased and corrupted one who promised well to discharge his duties.

What should we say to the Judge who addressed, or to the law which would allow a Judge to address an offender in these terms? "You are convicted of the high misdemeanour of offering for sale religious books without a license. We have taken into our humane consideration the mitigating circumstances of your case, your youth, your character, your inability to procure employment; and we sentence you to imprisonment in the House of Correction for one month. You shall there spend your days amongst the worst thieves with which this metropolis is infested; and your nights with those who are infected with a desperate and contagious disorder; taking lessons from the one of blasphemy and dissoluteness, and from the other imbibing the seeds of a disease which you shall carry home to your family. And we trust that, *taking advantage of the opportunities of reformation thus afforded you, and grateful that you live in a country which displays such tender interest in the present and permanent welfare of its erring subjects*, you will leave prison improved and corrected, knowing better your duty to God and to man, a respectable member of society, and a blessing to your parents."

Who could hear such a sentence without feelings of indignant derision, yet this sentence is virtually pronounced every week in this metropolis. It is not the fault of the acting magistrates, they are fully sensible of the corrupting consequences of imprisonment. I appeal to every one of them whether a week passes in which they are not reduced to this awkward dilemma; either they must encourage crime by allowing it to pass with impunity, or they must increase crime by the very punishment they inflict upon it. Another circumstance is equally perplexing to the magistrate in the country. A delinquent is brought before him, he gravely sentences him to a certain period of "hard labour" in the Bridewell, at the very moment he knows, the whole court knows, the culprit knows, that labour hard or light is not permitted in that House of Correction. Surely it is time that there should be some conformity between the letter and the execution of the law. This conflict should cease between the sentence and the reality. The farce of condemning a man to work, and compelling him to be idle, should no longer be acted in a grave judicial proceeding; either the Bridewell should be furnished with the means of hard labour, or the terms should be struck from the statute book, and "idleness" and "dissipation" be substituted.

Having thus added to the description of our jails some examples of their effect, I must close this chapter as I closed the detail of the Borough Compter, by leaving my readers to decide whether vice and misery are produced or prevented by our system of prison discipline.

It is a matter of much satisfaction to me to observe, that my opinions upon the subject of prison discipline, are confirmed by the high authority of "the Committee of Aldermen of London, appointed in 1815, to visit several jails in England, and directed to compare the allowances, and the rules and orders now existing in this City's prisons, with those of Gloucester, and elsewhere, and to draw out such new system of allowances, and such new code of laws as shall appear to them to be salutary, and adapted to the three prisons in question, *as likewise to the Borough Jail.*" Their report states, that certain alterations in the construction might be desirable; but as the difficulties of these would be great, and the expense enormous, they confine themselves to such alterations and improvements as they conceive may be attainable in the constructions of the prisons of this city.

Some of these attainable improvements are,—

1. That the jail should be divided into day-rooms, and distinct yards, having arcades in each.

2. That warm and cold baths should be provided, as also ovens, for fumigating clothes.

3. Circular apertures of open iron work, for the purpose of a thorough ventilation, should be made.

4. Such shutters and windows shall be constructed, as shall

exclude the possibility of the prisoners looking into any other apartment or yard.

5. That day-cells for labour should be distinct from the sleeping cells, as also exclusive cells for refractory prisoners.

6. King's evidence should be precluded from a possibility of communication with the other prisoners.

7. That gratings should be fitted up in the apartments where the visitors of felons are admitted; and so constructed, as not to admit of any dangerous instrument being passed through.

8. Apartments for the reception of friends of the debtors should be constructed.

9. The chapel should be so constructed, that one class of prisoners should not be seen by another class.

With respect to the classification of prisoners, according to their several degrees of offence:—

10. That those before trial should never be mixed with those convicted; and that the respective classes should be arranged as nearly as possible, in the following order:

1. Capital felons.
2. Simple felony, and first offence.
3. Criminals under sentence of death.
4. Misdemeanors, and persons wanting sureties.
5. Misdemeanors of the grossest kind.
6. Children.

With respect to the internal regulations of the prison:—

11. That all prisoners on coming in should be examined by

the Surgeon, and should be immediately washed, and their clothes purified; and proper apparel should be provided for their use in the mean time.

12. That the prisoners should be required to wash themselves, at least once every day, at places appropriated for that purpose; and that clean towels of open net-work be supplied for their use, twice a week.

13. That no beer should be admitted; nor wine, nor other strong liquors, except to the infirmaries, by direction of the Surgeon, or to the debtors. No debtor to be allowed to have to himself more than one pint of wine, or one quart of strong beer per day.

14. The friends of criminals to be admitted between the hours of nine in the morning, and two in the afternoon; and not to be allowed to converse with the prisoners, but in the presence of the keeper or turnkey, except solicitors for the purpose of preparing defences.

15. The visitors of debtors to be admitted only at stated hours, into the rooms allotted for their reception, and not into the interior of the jail, unless by order of a magistrate.

16. Not any description of prisoners should be permitted to enter into the sleeping-rooms during the day.

17. The transports, and those sentenced to hard labour or solitary confinement, to be kept in constant work suitable to their ability and strength: such prisoners not to be excused from work, unless on account of total inability, ill health, or other sufficient cause certified by the Surgeon.

18. Prisoners to be discharged in the morning, and if they have acquired any trade in the prison, proper tools to be given to them.

19. That gaming of every kind should be strictly prohibited.

With respect to the allowances of food:—

20. That one pound and a half of bread, at least one day old, should be allowed to each prisoner daily, and one pint of good gruel for breakfast,—and upon good behaviour half a pound of meat on a Sunday.

21. That proper scales, weights, and measures, should be provided in the jail.

22. A messenger to be appointed for the accommodation of the debtors.

23. A laundry, and a matron under whose directions the female prisoners should do all the washing.

24. A bell to be fixed for sounding alarms in cases of escape, and for other purposes.

25. The chaplain to keep a diary of observations, subject to the inspection of the visiting magistrates. He should read prayers, and preach a sermon every Sunday morning, and read prayers in the evening, and also read prayers every Wednesday and Friday. He should visit the sick, instruct prisoners in their moral duties, give spiritual advice, and religious consolation to such as may desire it. He should distribute amongst them religious books, and form a sort of school for the instruction of the children.

Besides the confirmation derived from the recorded opinions of the committee of Aldermen. I have an authority of the very highest order—the law of the land. It has been a matter of great satisfaction to me to find, that though the practices in prisons are most distressing and disgraceful, yet that they are as much against law as they are against reason and humanity. To the 19th Geo. III. c. 5. I would beg to direct the attention of every person who is interested in the subject of this book. It was framed by the late Lord Auckland, Judge Blackstone, and Mr. Howard: each of these gentlemen was distinguished by some peculiar and admirable characteristic. This statute combines and places in the fairest point of view, their respective excellencies, knowledge, discrimination, and philanthropy.

It would be tedious to my readers if I were now to abstract all the regulations relative to prisons; but I will mention a few as furnishing a curious contrast between the provisions of the law, and the manner of its present administration.

By 22d and 23d Charles II. c. 20. The jailer shall not put, keep, or lodge prisoners for debt and felons, together in one room or chamber; but they shall be put, kept, and lodged, separate and apart from one another in distinct rooms; on pain of forfeiting his office, and treble damages to the party grieved.

By 19th Charles II. c. 4. Whereas there is not yet any sufficient provision made for the relief, and setting on work poor and needy prisoners committed to the common jail for felony and other misdemeanors, *who many times perish before their trial; and the poor there living idle and unemployed become debauched, and come forth instructed in the practice of thievery and lewdness.* For remedy whereof, be it enacted, that the justices of the peace of the respective counties at any of their general sessions, or the major part of them then there assembled, if they shall find it needful so to do, may provide a stock of such materials as they find convenient for the setting poor prisoners on work, in such manner and by such ways as other county charges by the laws and statutes of the realm are and may be levied and raised; and to pay and provide fit persons to oversee, and to set such prisoners on work.

The 14th Geo. III. c. 59. states, " Whereas the malignant fever, commonly called the jail distemper, is found to be owing to want of cleanliness and fresh air in the several jails; the fatal consequences whereof might be prevented, if the justices of the peace were duly authorised to provide such accommodations in jails as may be necessary to answer this salutary purpose:—It is enacted that the justices shall order the walls of every room to be scraped and whitewashed once every year, &c.; and constantly supplied with hand ventilators or otherwise; *and shall order two rooms in each jail,—one for the men and one for the women, to be set apart for the sick prisoners, directing them to be removed into such rooms as soon as they shall be seized with any disorders, and kept separate from those who shall be in health;* and shall order a warm and cold bath, or commodious bathing tubs to be provided in each jail, and direct the prisoners to be washed in them, according to the condition in which they shall be at the time, before they are suffered to go out of the jail upon any occasion whatsoever."

By 31st Geo. III. c. 46. s. 5. "Two or more justices are appointed visitors of prisons; and such visiting justices shall *personally visit and inspect each such prison at least three times in each quarter of a year*, and oftener, if occasion shall require; and at every general or quarter sessions, the said visiting justices respectively shall make a report in writing of the state and condition of the said jail; and of all abuses which may occur to their observation therein."

24th Geo. III. c. 54. s. 4. "And be it further enacted, That the said Justices of the Peace, as well in the choice of the ground, as in determining upon the plans for building, re-building, enlarging, and altering such jails, as aforesaid, and the yards, courts, and outlets thereof, shall, as far as conveniently may be, pursue such measures, and adopt such plans as *shall provide separate and distinct places of confinement, and dry and airy* (1) *cells, in which the several prisoners of the following descriptions respectively, may be confined as well by day as by night; namely*, (2) *prisoners convicted of felony*, (3) *prisoners committed on charge or suspicion of felony*, (4) *prisoners committed for, or adjudged to be guilty of misdemeanors only*, (5) *and debtors*, (6) the females of each class to be separated from the females; and a separate place of confinement to be provided for such prisoners as are intended to be examined as (7) witnesses, on behalf of any prosecution of any indictment for felony; and also separate (8) infirmaries or sick wards for the men and (9) the women; and also a (10) chapel, and convenient (11) warm and cold baths, or bathing tubs, for the use of the prisoners, in such manner as is directed by an Act made in the 14th year of the reign of his present Majesty, intituled, An Act for preserving the Health of Prisoners in Jails, and preventing the Jail Distemper, and Care to be taken that the Prisoners shall not be kept in any Apartment under Ground.' " *

Now, urged by no motive but a sincere desire to rescue the wretches immured within the Borough Compter, from a continuance of their deplorable sufferings, I venture to recommend the Aldermen of London to visit that prison, with a copy of these, some of the propositions of their own committee in one hand, and the laws to which I have referred in the other. They will find, that not one of these regulations, deemed so desirable in 1815, are as yet attempted; and that each of these statutes, which the legislature, in its mercy has enacted, is positively violated.

I have already noticed the benevolence displayed by the legislature, in its provisions for the regulation of prisons; but their intentions will be, as they have hitherto been, of little avail, if they do not enforce them.

Some additions and alterations appear also desir-

* The Borough Compter alone furnishes eleven violations of this statute.

able; amongst the latter, I will mention that the law in some instances imposes, in case of non-performance of its regulations, a penalty on the jailer: for example, in case of mixing debtors with felons, the jailer is fined and dismissed from his office. But it may happen, and I have proved that it does happen in this metropolis, that the jailer has no option; he must break the law every day. He must either refuse to receive debtors, contrary to one statute; or he must place them in the yard to which female felons resort, contrary to another. If a penalty is to be imposed at all, surely it ought to be directed against those who have the power to obviate the outrage, and not against him who has none.

Amongst the additions which I will venture to recommend, are a clear and specific declaration of the law relative to irons on prisoners, their food and their clothing.

Nothing can be more capricious than the existing practice with regard to irons.

In *Chelmsford, and in Newgate*, all for felony are ironed.

At *Bury, and at Norwich*, all are without irons.*

At *Abingdon*, the untried are not ironed.

At *Derby*, none but the untried are ironed.

At *Cold-bath-fields*, none but the untried, and those sent for re-examination, are ironed.

At *Winchester*, all before trial are ironed; and those sentenced to transportation after trial:

* When I say none are ironed, it is to be understood, without they are refractory, or attempt to escape.

At *Chester*, those alone of bad character are ironed, whether tried or untried.

And there is as much variety in the weight of the fetters; some are heavy, others are light: in one prison they are placed on one leg, at another on both.

The quantum of food is equally variable.

Tothill Fields, and Ipswich.—No allowance for debtors except from charity.

Bedford, three quartern loaves per week.

Bristol, a four-penny loaf per day.

Borough Compter, fourteen ounces of bread per day, two pounds of meat per week.

Bury, one pound and a half of bread per day, one pound of cheese, and three-quarters of a pound of meat per week.

Norwich, two pound of bread per day, half a pound of cheese per week.

Penitentiary, Milbank,—one pound and a half of bread, one pound of potatoes, two pints of hot gruel, per day, and either six ounces of boiled meat, without bone, or a quart of strong broth mixed with vegetables.

Fourteen ounces of bread per day, with two pounds of meat per week, are not enough to support life; besides, in some prisons, the allowance is withheld for a considerable time. The hour of delivery is fixed, and if a prisoner arrives after it, he receives nothing till the next morning. Persons may steal for immediate sustenance. I do not contend that they are not criminal. True morality would tell them it is better to starve than to rob; but in truth, such a sacrifice of life to principle, is an effort of heroic virtue; and, perhaps, if those amongst ourselves, who, free from every temptation, call aloud for rigid and inflexible justice, were placed in the same circumstances, they would have some difficulty in the choice of the alternative, and hunger might make appeals which honesty could hardly reject.

There are differences with regard to bedding:—

From—No bedding, or coverlid,
A blanket for two men,
A blanket for each,
Two blankets for each,
Two blankets and a rug each,
Three blankets and a rug for each,
To, three blankets, a rug, a hair bed, and two pillows each.

The same dissimilarity exists in clothing. Some prisons provide a dress, others do not; some prisoners are comfortably clad, and some are almost naked.

One general observation will apply to all these varieties of treatment. Parity of crime ought not to meet with disparity of punishment; and it seems hardly just, that, if a man commits an offence on one bank of a stream, which separates two counties, he should be chained and half starved—if on the other bank, he should be well fed, well clothed, and exempt from bodily suffering.

It is the chief boast and glory of Great Britain,

that equal justice is administered to all, but it must surely be admitted, that an exception to this exists, while imprisonment is relaxed, or aggravated, not according to the degree of crime, nor according to any certain rule or standard.

PART II.

Non fortia loquor, sed possibilia.

IF I have been so fortunate as to convince my readers, that crime and misery are the natural and necessary consequences of our present system of prison discipline. I must now endeavour to demonstrate, that these may be avoided. I do nothing, I freely admit, if I shew that these evils exist, without proving that they might have been prevented. I may be answered thus:—It is true, that our jails are nurseries, schools, and colleges of vice;—true, our prisoners are rendered miserable as well as guilty;—true, their health and morals are tainted; but guilt and wretchedness are the inseparable concomitants of confinement, and must ever be so.

To prove that the reverse of all this is true,—that instead of health being impaired, it may be improved; that instead of morals being corrupted, they may be reformed; that these objects, so desirable to the state, may be accomplished by methods humane to the criminal, by a system of classification, industry, and religious instruction, is the design of the Second Part of this Pamphlet; and, abstaining from abstract reasoning, I shall appeal to experience and example.

Bury Jail,

AND

House of Correction.*

THIS Jail is the best constructed, of any that I have seen in England, the regulations by which it is governed are exceedingly wise and humane; and it possesses the grand requisite of a Governor, who discharges his duty with equal zeal and fidelity.

The nature of the building will be easily understood. An external wall surrounds the whole: the Governor's house is in the center; from its windows every yard is visible, and it is hardly possible, that any breach of the rules can be practised without being observed, either by himself or some one of his family. He told me that the experience of twenty years as a jailer, had taught him that the main points for prison discipline, for the security, morals, and health of the prisoners, are:—

Classification—Employment—and Cleanliness.

Classification is carried to almost its greatest limit. There is a separate building and yard, for prisoners of the following descriptions:—

Males.

No. 1 and 2. Debtors.

3. King's Evidence, when there are any; and occasionally other prisoners.

* Visited, January, 1818.

4. Convicted of misdemeanors, and small offences.
5. Transports, and convicted of atrocious felonies.
6. Untried for atrocious offences.
7. Untried for small offences.

Females.

8. Debtors.
9. For trial.
10. Convicted of misdemeanors.*
11. Convicted of felonies.*

There is a well merited discretion given to the Governor, to alter these rules, in the following manner:—a notorious thief, who has before been imprisoned, may be apprehended for a petty offence. To place him amongst petty offenders is to subject them to corruption. He is, therefore, confined with the untried for "atrocious offences." On the other hand, a youth of respectable habits, evidently unhardened in guilt, may be charged with an atrocious offence; he is placed amongst the untried for small offences.

It is to be observed that there is no separation of boys from men, or of untried women, whether their offences are small or great; but the building appropriated for King's evidence, may generally be devoted to the confinement of boys.

The prison is calculated to hold eighty-four persons, and there are eighty-four separate sleeping

* These are in a detached house of correction.

cells, consequently each person, when they have only that number, sleeps by himself, which the Governor thinks a regulation of great importance. But at present there are considerably more:—it is, therefore, necessary to place more than one in a room, and the Governor, in these cases, places three together; having had reason to apprehend that two, sleeping in the same cell, are productive of mischief.

Health is preserved and improved by the cleanliness of person, apartments, and yards.

Prisoners, when they arrive, have their hair cut short, and this is so continued. They must wash well every morning, and do not receive their allowance till this is done. There are cold and warm baths.

Prisoners are shaved every Saturday, and put on clean linen (provided if necessary by the County) on the Sunday; each day-room, work-room, and cell, is swept every morning, and washed twice a-week in the summer, and once in the winter; and the passages, apartments, and cells, are white washed after each assize. Prisoners, when they enter, are examined; if necessary, they go into the warm bath, and at night their clothes are baked; and, if they appear ragged, they are provided with plain clothes at the expense of the County.

Employment.

When an untried prisoner comes in, it is at his option whether he will work: if he is inclined, any work to which he has been accustomed is provided, if possible; and to encourage his labour, the whole amount of his earnings is given to him.

The earnings of the convicts are divided in the following manner:—one-fifth to the Governor, two-fifths to the County, two-fifths to the prisoner, of which he receives half, and half is reserved till his departure. Then also sufficient is given him to carry him home, and a small sum to support him, till he can look out for work.

That part of the money, which is received in prison, may be thus expended. One of the porters goes round twice a-week, and writes down those things which the prisoners wish to purchase. This list, sometimes amounting to 200 articles, is submitted to the Governor, who puts his pen through those, which he deems improper. He then orders the others, and the prisoners receive them at cost price, and have weights, scales, and measures, to satisfy themselves as to the quantity. All spirituous liquors are strictly forbidden.

The work consists in making clothes, shoes, list-shoes, straw-hats, &c.; and grinding at a mill, of a peculiar construction, somewhat similar to a turn-spit. They walk in rows, and the machine is turned rather by their weight than their exertions. The advantage is, that no man can avoid his share of labour. This mill is worked by gangs, above and below, who are also classified, and if there are not sufficient of one description, the number is made up by drafts from another; but under the following judicious regulations:—if the number of convicts of heinous offences is not sufficient, the most atrocious in crime, or the most depraved in character, from the misdemeanants, are added; on the other hand, if the number of misdemeanants is too small, it is made up from the most orderly of the criminal ward.

Under the article health, I omitted to mention that the jail is distant about half a mile from the town, and stands in a dry, and airy situation, and every precaution is taken to ventilate the rooms. This, the Governor deems very important, as he has found that the prisoners consider that comfort consists in closeness, and would, if permitted, exclude all air. He finds the prisoners grow fat and improve in health; and, this he ascribes to exercise, cleanliness, and the absence of stimulating liquors.

Irons are never used but as a punishment.

The beds are of iron; a straw palliasse, two blankets, and a rug. The food is, for untried, one pound and a half of bread per day, and one pound of cheese per week; with an addition of one pound of meat per week for convicts, whose work at the mill is hard, and, therefore, requires further nourishment. It was formerly the practice to dress their meat, and to furnish them with soups, but, at the request of the Governor, this has been discontinued, as he finds it necessary for the purpose of giving a proper moral influence to the Governor, that he should be, not only above fraud, but above the suspicion of it; and this suspicion might be generated, if they do not receive their provisions in a raw state.

There is an infirmary in every ward, and bibles and

prayer books. The Governor seldom goes round without being solicited for permission to learn to read and write.

This is accomplished by giving small rewards to those in each ward who have capacity and inclination to teach others. Almost all, therefore, who remain any length of time, learn these important accomplishments, and he always has found a great avidity in the prisoners to be instructed.

Almost every man who remains after conviction, learns some trade, which may hereafter be an aid to his family, if it does not become his regular business; for instance, all the convicts for atrocious crimes have learned to make list shoes, and straw hats. This trade they exercise in the intervals when they are not employed at the mill, and they contrive to earn for themselves, from one to about three shillings per week. The Governor thinks that prisoners ought not to be employed, merely or principally as a speculation of profit; because, the produce of such labour, from fluctuations in its value, and from the inexpertness of the workmen, may often be very inconsiderable: but he deems it a matter of vital importance, that they should be employed, from the moral effect produced. If there were no gain, if there were a loss by their labour, he would still employ them and pay them for their work, as the only method of avoiding disturbances, improving their character, and insuring their security.

He thinks that no general rules relative to solitary confinement ought to be made, because of its different effect on different people. Some years ago he had two men, (as he thinks) from the same farm yard, condemned to solitary confinement; one a stupid sluggish fellow, slept away his time; the other an active, energetic man, was almost driven out of his senses, so much so, as to render it necessary to relax his punishment.

His experience has led him to approve of labour, not only as contributing to the security and morals, but also to the comfort of prisoners. He lately had occasion to punish one ward, which he did by depriving them of the materials of extra labour, and not a day passed in which he did not receive solicitations for its return, and promises of amendment. He lately received from a neighbouring workhouse, a woman who was guilty of very outrageous conduct, and absolutely refused to do any work, the Governor was requested to do his utmost for her reformation: he confined her alone without work, and while I was there, she solicited a wheel in the most urgent manner, saying, employment would ease her mind, and help her to while away the time.

As for their conduct after they leave prison, he has repeatedly had persons who have before been confined, call upon him to thank him for the lessons they had learnt in prison: he knows many who were dissolute characters before, who immediately on leaving prison have gone to honest labour, and are now industrious and respectable men.

Masters have thanked him for the reformation of

their servants; one within this week assured him, that a boy, who, before his imprisonment, was of the most abandoned character, has since become quite an example to his other labourers.

Two young men were confined for the same offence; he lately saw a letter from one to a comrade in prison, describing his own mal-practices, with considerable exultation; but, saying, as for George, (the other) he has turned out quite a fool, he works all the week, goes to church on a Sunday, and will not speak to his old acquaintance. The father of this lad, who has thus deserted his former practices and accomplices, called in the interval of my two visits, to express his thankfulness; his words were, as for the boy, it is salvation to him, and poor as I am, it is worth more than a hundred pounds to me: I wish he had been with you five years ago.

He believes that no serious misconduct in any way could take place, without some of the prisoners giving him information;—lately, the turnkey was called up by the prisoners, to tell him that they heard a man endeavouring to escape, and he found him attempting to cut the windows of his cell.

He does not allow any gaming, or chucking halfpence, which he prevents by requiring the ward to inform him if it takes place, and confining them all for the day, if he discovers it.

He observed, that the rules of a prison ought not to be too severe, but rigidly enforced; as simple as possible, for if they were intricate, if the concern did not move mechanically, it would soon get out of order.

He observed also, that it was plain justice to treat an untried prisoner with as little restraint as possible.

Such are the rules of this prison, and such the results of the experience of the Governor: if the health of a prisoner, his security, and the prevention of crime, be important matters in the conduct of a jail, the following facts speak for themselves.

There is no prisoner at this time ill.

In eighteen years but one prisoner has escaped, and he in the middle of the day, and in double irons.

In every hundred prisoners, there are not five who have been here before. At this moment out of one hundred and thirty, there are seven of such, also four for atrocious offences, and three for assaults, or petty misdeeds.

He never has riots, or quarrelling, or swearing.

This jail reflects the highest credit on the magistrates of the district, and they receive from their humane labours, the most important advantages.

I left this account with the Governor for a week, that he might correct any inaccuracies; he confirmed every thing which is here stated, but insisted on my suppressing a paragraph at the end, in which I had expressed my opinion of his conduct.

The Maison de Force, at Ghent.*

THIS prison is situated just out of the city. It was originally intended to be an octagon, but at present only five departments are finished;—still an entire separation is effected between,

Men and women,
The sickly and the healthy,
The untried and the convicted,
Misdemeanants and felons.

It is in contemplation to finish the building, and when this takes place, there will be six additional subdivisions. For each of the above description of prisoners, an open court is provided, in which they have their daily exercise.

First we saw the untried, and those who have appealed against their sentences. There is nothing peculiar in their treatment. They do not work, and no instruction is afforded to them.

We next visited the tried. Their beds are in small recesses, from a gallery opening to the court. Each has a separate sleeping cell, which is furnish-

* I visited this prison in November, 1817. I have since sent to the Governor a copy of this statement, with questions upon some points, of which I was doubtful, but as yet I have not received his answer.

ed with a metal bedstead, a thick mattress, a double sheet, a double and single blanket, and a pillow. The bedding is brought out to be aired in fine weather, and the doors are open all day. The rooms were perfectly sweet and clean.

The major part of the prisoners of the same class work together, in rooms 170 feet long and 26 broad. The principal employment is weaving calico, damask, and sacking cloth, but there are shops for sawyers, carpenters, blacksmiths, &c.

The utmost order and regularity are preserved. No prisoner is allowed to speak, and to such an extent was this carried, that they did not answer our questions, when we addressed them. I never saw any manufactory, in which the workmen were more busy; whenever we went, there was no noise but the motion of the shuttle; and every eye and every hand was engaged. Whether our conductor was with us, or at a distance, no difference was observable. In fact, order was carried to its highest point.

This manufactory is under a contractor, who furnishes each prisoner daily, with twenty-six ounces of brown bread, and two quarts of soup, for which he receives from government three-pence half-penny per head. He provides raw materials: these are weighed when they are given out, and when they are returned, and the prisoner must pay for any deficiency. He also finds machinery, but the person who uses it, is answerable for any accident. The work done is estimated according to a regulated price, and the prisoner receives the whole amount of his earnings every week. The contractor appoints from among the prisoners two or more overseers in each room, whose duty it is, to inspect the operations of the others, and to preserve silence.

In each court there is a canteen, opened at stated hours, three times per day. The Governor stands beside it; the prisoners are arranged in rows, and are brought up to it, two at a time. Each article is spread upon a table before them, with the price attached to it, they take what they choose, put down the money, and retire to make room for the next pair.

The goods sold are thus under the inspection of the Governor; the venders also take an oath, not to sell any prohibited article, amongst which, are all fermented liquors. By these regulations every thing improper is effectually excluded.

The priest, with assistants, performs mass on a Sunday. On other days his duty is confined to the sick, and those under sentence of death; but, as premeditated murder is the only capital crime in these countries, the number of the latter is very inconsiderable.

The infirmary has a garden attached to it, for the use of the sick. There are various separate rooms and yards, for those who have infectious disorders, and the remainder occupy an apartment seventy feet long, and about thirty broad, which is perfectly ventilated by windows, and valves in the ceiling. The number of the sick did not exceed twenty-five. The whole number of prisoners was rather more than thirteen hundred. To our question—" Out of one hundred persons, released from this prison, how many return here? The sub-jailer replied, about five. In answer to the same question, the Governor said,—That "of the felons, ten per cent. return, but hardly any of the misdemeanants." There is then no essential variation in their accounts. We did not see a fetter, or a chain, in the whole prison. The refractory are sentenced to prohibition of work, or to solitary confinement, not exceeding ten days. In former times corporal punishment was allowed, but this is now dispensed with—"merely," as the Governor said, "because it was found to be unnecessary." Privation of work is penalty sufficient to keep ninety-nine out of a hundred, orderly and attentive to the rules; and if they do occasionally receive one of an unusually turbulent and ungovernable disposition, a week's solitary confinement invariably reduces him to obedience,—a repetition of this effectual and dreaded mode of discipline, is an event of very rare occurrence.

The mode of treatment of a prisoner, is:

Before his trial he is merely confined, he is not compelled to work, but if he wishes it he is provided with the materials; he is furnished with a sufficiency of food and clothing, has a well ventilated cell for the night, and a large airy yard and covered corridors for his exercise and recreation by day; and he has no communication with convicts, or with delinquents suspected of crimes of a different degree of atrocity from that with which he is charged. He can see his friends or legal advisers at certain hours, and under certain regulations, and if his health is impaired, he receives every accommodation, and the best medical attendance.

When he is convicted, he is immediately introduced to the manufactory; if he understands any kind of work which is practised in it, he is furnished with the tools, &c.; if he is ignorant, he is placed as an apprentice to some experienced workman, who is interested in his instruction, as for a certain period he receives a portion of his earnings.

The same care of his diet, health, and cleanliness, is continued; he is allowed two hours exercise, and the remainder of the day is devoted to hard labour. By this excellent system he gains habits of order, self-restraint, and subjection of mind; diligence becomes habitual, and is rendered agreeable by the wages it produces. At present he receives the whole amount of his earnings, but this is a new and a bad arrangement; and it is intended to revert to the old plan, by which one third was reserved for his use on his departure. Many instances have occurred within the Governor's recollection, of persons acquiring two or three hundred francs; and at this time he knows many tradesmen in Ghent, who, on leaving prison, had set up in the business which they had thus learned, had been enabled to do so by the capital they had thus saved, and had flourished by those habits of industry which they had thus acquired. Mr. Howard illustrates the effects of the system of labour by this anecdote.—" I have heard, that a countryman of ours, who was a prisoner in the Rasp-house at Amsterdam several years, was permitted to work at his own trade, shoemaking; and by being constantly kept employed, was quite cured of the vices that were the cause of his confinement. My informant added, that the prisoner received at his release a surplus of his earnings, which enabled him to set up his trade in London, where he lived in credit, and at dinner commonly drank, 'Health to his worthy masters at the Rasp-house.'"

Nothing in the whole institution struck me so much as the subdued, civil, submissive, decent behaviour of all the prisoners. There was a degree of cleanliness in their persons, and an air of cheerfulness in their countenances: in short, an appearance of comfort and respectability which was the strongest evidence of the success of the system. I had lately visited the principal prison of our own metropolis, and I can convey no adequate conception of the contrast. The most boisterous tempest is not more distinct from the serenity of a summer's evening: the wildest beast of prey is not more different from our domesticated animals, than is the noise, contention, licentiousness, and tumult of Newgate, from the quietness, industry, and regularity of the Maison de Force.

It is very remarkable that Mr. Howard saw this prison in 1775, and 1778, and speaks of the "good institution," in high terms of commendation. He notices the industry that prevailed: I was present, he says, during the whole time the men prisoners were at dinner, and much admired the regularity, decency, and order with which the whole was conducted. Every thing was done at a word, given by a director; no noise or confusion appeared, and this company of stout criminals was governed with as much apparent ease, as the most sober and well disposed assembly in civil society.

In 1785, he visited it again, and found "a great alteration for the worse; the flourishing and useful manufactory destroyed; the looms and utensils all sold, in consequence of the Emperor's too hasty attention to a petition from a few interested persons. That which ought to be the leading view in all such houses, is now lost in this house. Many formerly ascribed the comfort and happiness of their lives to the trades here learned, and the attention here paid to them; but now, the men and women do not earn, one with another, seven farthings a day. Their victuals are also reduced; the meat, from half a pound to six ounces, and greens from three to two farthings worth a day. Their bread, made in the house, is now ammunition bread. In consequence of this vile policy I found the aspect of the prisoners quite changed; nor could I wonder to hear that *a quarter of the house is soon to be fitted up for an infirmary.*"

Prison of Philadelphia.*

"May the New Continent, accustomed to receive from Europe, that illumination which her youth and inexperience require, serve, in her turn, as a Model to reform the Criminal Jurisprudence, and establish a new system of imprisonment in the Old World;—severe and terrible, yet humane and just."

DUKE DE LIANCOURT.

ABOUT the year 1776, the prisons in America were in a situation very similar to that of the generality of English prisons at the present moment. There was no such thing as classification, employment, instruction or cleanliness: arbitrary rule and brutality, fetters put on, or withdrawn according to wanton caprice, oaths and invectives indiscriminately dealt out, were the only methods of discipline; but these severities "were in some sense amply compensated to the prisoners, by the permission of debauchery and excess; by the liquors they were allowed to purchase, and the indolence in which they were indulged." Filth, drunkenness, irregularity, and promiscuous intercourse, produced the same effects in American, as they now produce in English jails. Disease was very prevalent; crime increased,

* This description is compiled from various publications upon the subject, and from the communications of a gentleman who is one of the committee for alleviating the distresses of prisoners in Philadelphia.

and "scarcely one was dismissed from prison with the same stock of morality he carried in with him."

A few benevolent persons in Pennsylvania, deeply deploring these evils, formed themselves into "a society for alleviating the miseries of public prisons." After fourteen years of labour and disappointment, they succeeded in obtaining liberty from the legislature to introduce *by way of experiment*, an arrangement, in which the classification of crime, and the employment of the criminal, were the most important features. A host of adversaries to the alteration immediately sprung up; prejudice was very widely dispersed; the new mode of discipline and its projectors were subjects of general derision; their motives were suspected, and the certain failure of their plans was predicted. The jailers pronounced them impracticable; the Judges, with one exception, were decidedly adverse, and the government so far yielded to popular opinion as to limit the operation of the new system, to a period of five years. No time was lost in making the necessary alterations in the building; and the experiment was commenced; but here a new difficulty arose. The prisoners had been taught to believe that the regulations were injurious to them; nor is this to be wondered at, for nothing appears more grievous to a person long practised in habits of indolence and licentiousness, than the idea of being compelled to alter them; a conspiracy instigated by the jailer, for a breach of prison, was formed, and was carried into execution on the day on which the operations of the society began.

By the time the five years of probation had elapsed, the current of public favour had entirely turned. Not one man in America, says the Duke De Liancourt, doubted the efficacy of the system; the Judges were its most strenuous supporters. It was made a permanent law, and the example of Philadelphia has been followed in the States of New York, Virginia, Massachusetts, Vermont, Connecticut, New Jersey, and Maryland.

I will now proceed to a detail of the system.

The prisoners are divided into the following classes.

1. The untried.
2. Convicts for atrocious crimes.
3. Convicts for lesser offences.
4. Vagrants.
5. Debtors.

And there is no communication between men and women.

The untried are not forced to work, but they are furnished with materials and implements if they desire them.

There are, a manufactory of nails at which about five hundred weight are daily made; extensive blacksmiths' and carpenters' sheds; shops furnished with instruments and tools for joiners, turners, shoemakers, tailors, weavers of cloth, linen, and carpetting.

In the yard, the employments are sawing and polishing marble, cutting stone, and rasping logwood.

There is a mill for grinding corn; and another for preparing plaster of Paris.

All these various avocations are carried on with the utmost order and activity; there was, says Mr. Turnbull, such a spirit of industry visible on every side; and such contentment pervaded the countenances of all, that it was with difficulty I divested myself of the idea, that these men surely were not convicts, but accustomed to labour from their infancy."

An account is opened with every prisoner; he is debited with the amount of the sum stolen, or embezzled; with the expenses of his prosecution; with the fine imposed by the court; with the cost of his board and clothes; and he is credited with the produce of his labour. This account is furnished to him quarterly; at the expiration of his appointed term of imprisonment, if there remains a balance against him, he is retained till it is liquidated by his earnings; if a balance in his favour, he receives it. Thus idleness at one period must be compensated by redoubled industry at another; a certain quantity of work must be performed, and it becomes his interest to accomplish this as speedily as possible; because the shorter the period of his confinement, the less are the deductions for board and clothing. Besides, a report from the inspectors, of his good conduct and industry, seldom fails to induce the prosecutor to forego a part of his claim; and the government, to remit the fine, and to abridge the term of his sentence. These representations however are made with great caution; the prisoner must have conducted himself with propriety, must have evinced a subdued and penitent disposition, must have been constant at his work; in short he must for a long period have displayed symptoms of rea and permanent reformation, before he is considered to merit any intercession: and yet in spite of these precautions against indiscreet lenity, which are faithfully adhered to, the case of a man fulfilling the whole extent of his sentence, is an event of such rare occurrence, that my informant, in a period of ten years' attention to the concerns of the prison, could not call to his recollection a single instance of it.

When a convicted prisoner is received, a report is sent with him of the circumstances of his crime, particularly those which tend to palliate or to aggravate it, with other information as to his former character, and his conduct on his trial. He is then fully instructed in the rules of the prison; and at this period especially no pains are spared to awaken in his mind a sense of his guilt—the injury done thereby to society which protected him—the forfeit he has made of that protection—and the necessity of making compensation by his example and amendment.—Every encouragement is then given him to perform his duty with alacrity—to observe a decency of conduct towards his keeper and companions, and he is allowed to entertain a hope that a long and uninterrupted course of good behaviour will not pass unnoticed; but will procure for him an enlargement before the expiration of his term.*

He is then examined by the Surgeon, washed and clothed in a dress, which (as well as every mattress, sheet, rug, and coverlid,) is woven by the male, and made up by the female prisoners.

He is then appointed to any labour with which

* Turnbull.

he is acquainted; or being ignorant, he is instructed in some mode of employment.

A master-manufacturer attends his class, and superintends his work. The most orderly of the class is selected as monitor; who must render an account of any breach of rule. During the hours of labour, no prisoner is allowed to leave his work without permission. All laughing, singing, and conversation, except such as may immediately relate to the business in hand, are prohibited; and "the silence which is observed is the first and most striking circumstance which arrests the attention of a stranger."

Of the twelve inspectors, who are selected from the most respectable inhabitants of the town, and who act gratuitously, one visits the prison every day: he discourses with those whom he thinks most capable of being moved by his exhortations, apart from the rest.

Great attention is paid to the promotion of moral and religious improvement, by a supply of useful books, and by the regular performance of divine service, at which all the prisoners are required to attend.

For breakfast they have three-fourths of a pound of good bread, with molasses and water; at dinner, half a pound of bread and beef, a bowl of soup and potatoes; sometimes herrings in the spring. At supper, corn, meal mash, and molasses, and sometimes boiled rice.

The only beverage is molasses and water. No provisions are permitted to be sent to the convicts from without.

The prisoners rise at dawn, and after making their

beds and washing themselves, commence their labour by sunrise. Intervals for relaxation and food are allowed in the course of the day, and at the approach of dusk a bell rings. Their work then concludes; they retire to their rooms, and form themselves in such a manner, that the keeper can have a perfect view of each. He counts them, and calls over the roll; half an hour is then allowed for the adjustment of their bedding, after which they are not permitted to speak aloud, or to make any noise.

Four watchmen, in their turns, patrole the passages through the night, and report any remarkable occurrence in the morning.

No keeper is permitted to carry a stick, or any offensive weapon.—There are neither fetters or irons belonging to the prison.

If any offence is committed against the internal regulations, the culprit is admonished; upon a repetition, he is excluded from the prisoners' table at dinner, and deprived of meat: if he still continue incorrigible, he is sentenced to a certain period of solitude.

There is not, probably, any degree of personal severity, which produces so powerful an impression upon the human mind, as solitary confinement. Its effect in the Philadelphia prison has been invariable: without one exception, those who have been subjected to this dreaded discipline, have returned to their labour with remarkable regularity. No instance has occurred of its being necessary to inflict it upon the same man twice.

The prisoner who is sentenced to this punishment, is confined in a narrow cell; his allowance of food is much diminished; the turnkey brings it to him in the morning, and retires without speaking a word. Thus condemned to his own thoughts, he has an opportunity of reviewing his past misconduct; and its folly, if not its wickedness, are before him. While his body is reduced by the scantiness of his diet, his mind is unsupported by the stimulants of society, in short, *he must reflect.* A few days are hardly elapsed, before a change is visible; and the proudest spirit will solicit enlargement, with promises of the utmost industry and quietness; and it is observed, that those who for violence and insubordination are once subjected to it, become the least troublesome of the prisoners.

Formerly in Pennsylvania, death was the penalty for a variety of offences; but, in the year 1791, a change in the penal code took place, and, with the exception of premeditated murder, every crime, heretofore capital, is punished by a period of imprisonment; a certain portion of which is to be passed in solitary confinement. This alteration, and the amendments in the mode of prison discipline, have produced an effect beyond the expectation of their most sanguine supporters.

Having thus described the plans which have been adopted in Philadelphia, (which, encountering much opposition and prejudice at their outset, have won the approbation of every person in the United States who is competent to judge of them: (plans which are now looked upon throughout America as axioms of indubitable truth, in the science of political economy; which alone, in a country where every other topic, government, politics, religion, are debated and contested, have received the testimony of universal assent; plans, too, which have been confirmed and approved by an experience of twenty-five years.) It only remains, that I say something as to their effects.

I have opportunities of personal communication with American gentlemen, who have devoted much of their time to the management of prisons; I have before me a variety of publications descriptive of that in Philadelphia; and it is remarkable, that persons the most opposite in their habits and modes of thinking,—the Duke de Liancourt,—Brissot,—members of the religious Society of Friends,—all concur in expressing their astonishment at the cleanliness of the prison, the composure and decency of the prisoners, the cheerfulness with which they labour, and the reformation which is produced upon them.

But, besides this ocular testimony, we have some important facts:—

"The effects of the new system have been seen in no particular more evidently, than in the diminution of disease among the convicts."

"The physician's bill, which formerly amounted from two hundred to three hundred and twenty dollars per quarter, at present seldom rises above forty."*

In the four years preceding the commencement of the new system, 104 prisoners escaped; † in the four succeeding, (except on the day of its establishment) not one escaped.

* Duke de Liancourt.

† Bradford.

But the most extraordinary manifestation of the efficacy of the alterations, is the decreased number of crimes, and the decreased atrocity of those which are committed. The Duke de Liancourt gives us the following table.—

CRIMES.	From January, 1787, to June, 1791, under the old system.	From June, 1791, to March, 1795, under the present system.
Murder	9	0
Manslaughter	0	5
Robbery	37	3
Burglary	77	16
Larceny	374	163
Forgery	5	10
Counterfeiting	6	4
Misdemeanor, 1st degree	4	3
Ditto, 2nd degree	13	1
Receiving stolen Goods, 1st deg.	26	1
Ditto Ditto 2nd deg.	6	5
Horse Stealing	10	27
Defrauding	3	3
Bigamy	1	0
Violent Assault to kill	6	0
Harbouring Convicts	5	0
Disorderly Houses	10	2
	592	243

Mr. Turnbull thus extracts the most heinous offences.—

CRIMES.	Under the old system in the city and county.	Under the new system in the whole state.
Burglary	77	16
Robbery	39	5
Murder	9	0
Arson	3	1
Rape	0	1
Bigamy	1	1
	129	24

It is to be observed, that during the four first of these eight years, the prisons were peopled from the city and county of Philadelphia alone; during the last four, the whole state of Pennsylvania had sent its convicts in addition.

The comparison of the number of persons who were for the second time sent to jail, is equally striking. Of the 594 crimes in the first period, 346 were perpetrated by 184 persons,* or upwards of 40 in a hundred were again re-committed; on the second, two in a hundred, was found to be the average number of those who returned to prison after being released from it.† It appears, however, that this proportion is somewhat increased, as 5 per cent. is now considered the fair estimate.

The following facts, which were originally given on the authority of Mr. Caleb Lownes, are instances of the effects of the system; and I insert them, though they have been repeatedly before the public, as they may not have fallen into the hands of some of my readers.

"At the time of the yellow fever, in 1793, great difficulty was found in obtaining nurses and attendants for the sick at Bush-hill hospital. Recourse was had to the prison. The request was made, and the apparent danger stated to the convicts. As many offered as were wanted.—They continued faithful till the dreadful scene was closed—none of them making a demand for their services, till all were discharged.

"One man committed for a burglary, who had seven years to serve, observed, when the request was made to him, that having offended society, he

* Bradford. † Duke de Liancourt.

would be happy to render it some services for the injury; and if they could only place a confidence in him, he would go with cheerfulness. He went—he never left it but once, and then by permission to obtain some articles in the city. His conduct was so remarkable as to engage the attention of the managers, who made him a deputy-steward; gave him the charge of the doors, to prevent improper persons from going into the hospital, to preserve order in and about the house, and to see that nothing came to or went from it improperly. He was paid, and after receiving an extra compensation, at his discharge married one of the nurses. Another man, convicted of a robbery, was taken out for the purpose of attending a horse and cart, to bring such provisions from the vicinity of the city, as were there deposited for the use of the poor, by those who were afraid to come in. He had the sole charge of the cart and conveying the articles, for the whole period. He had many years to serve, and might at any time have departed with the horse, cart, and provisions. He despised, however, such a breach of trust, and returned to the prison. He was soon after pardoned, with the thanks of the inspectors.

" Another instance of the good conduct of the prisoners during the sickness, happened among the women. When request was made of them to give up their bedsteads, for the use of the sick at the hospital, they *cheerfully offered* even their bedding, &c. When a similar request was made to the debtors, they *all refused*.

" A criminal, one of the desperate gangs that had

so long infested the vicinity of Philadelphia, for several years before the alteration of the system, on being discharged, called upon one of the inspectors, and addressed him in the following manner: 'Mr. ——, I have called to return you my thanks, for your kindness to me while under sentence, and to perform a duty which I think I owe to society, it being all in my power at this time to afford. You know my conduct and my character have been once bad and lost, and therefore whatever I might say would have but little weight was I not now at liberty. Pursue your present plan, you will have neither burglaries nor robberies in this place.' He then stated the sentiments held by those characters who had devoted themselves to this mode of life, and the plans generally pursued by them. The certainty of conviction and the execution of the sentence—the *privations*, temperance, order, labour, &c. was more to be dreaded than any thing they had ever experienced. He observed at parting, that he should never trouble the inspectors more. This promise has been fully complied with."

Penitentiary, Millbank.*

THIS house of correction, on which it is proposed to expend nearly 600,000*l.* is built in a morass. On going towards it, we observed a line, marking the height to which the water occasionally rises; consequently the foundations have hitherto been found entirely defective. The external wall gave way during the time it was building; two towers have al ready been taken down to prevent their falling; and two more are in a precarious state. Large external cracks are every where visible, and internally the ceilings are separating.† The state of the cells, the fissures in the wall, and the derangement of the pavement, seemed to us to warrant alarm, as to the permanence of the building. I mention these circumstances, because I anticipate very considerable and continual expense in its support; and this expense may be confounded with the inevitable charges of the penitentiary system; and thus a pre-

* With S. Hoare, jun. Esq. Dec. 26, 1817; and on Feb. 21, 1818, in company with Mr. W. Allen, I read this to the Governor, with a request that any errors might be pointed out.

† This was in December. I understand they have since been repaired.

judice may arise against it. But it is obvious, that the system can have nothing to do with any errors as to the situation which is chosen. It surely is not necessary always to select a swamp for the site of a building, which requires above all things a dry foundation, and a free wholesome atmosphere.

When a prisoner is brought here, he is first placed in the reception room, and examined by the surgeon; he is then bathed, and his clothes, if unfit to be preserved, are burnt; if decent, they are sold, and entered to his credit, in the "Prisoner's Property Book." He then is placed in the first class, and while he remains in it, he works in the cell in which he sleeps, separate from all other prisoners. When he is advanced to the second class, he performs his work in the larger cells, in company. If he is in the first, he may be advanced to the second, when he merits this indulgence; or being in the second, he may be degraded to the first, for misbehaviour. A regulation in the same spirit, allows a diminution of the period of his sentence, upon a favourable representation from the committee.

The hours of work are about nine, and the produce of his labour is thus divided—in every pound,

	s.	*d.*
The establishment has	15	0
The prisoner	2	6
The master-manufacturer	0	10
The taskmaster of the pentagon	0	10
The turnkeys of the pentagon	0	10
	20	0

The prisoner's money is placed to his credit, and it is either reserved, to be given him on his departure, or he is allowed to send it to his family; and a statement of his account is furnished to him.

There is a master-manufacturer, who is acquainted with the nature of such manufactures as are introduced; he directs all contracts for materials, has the custody of them, receives them from the prisoners in the shape of goods, and is responsible for all deficiencies.

There is a taskmaster for every pentagon, who superintends the work of the prisoners, and instructs those who are ignorant.

A prison dress is provided, and each class is distinguished by different clothing.

The diet for men daily, is one pound and a half of bread, one pound of potatoes, a pint of hot porridge for breakfast, and the same for supper, and either 6 ounces of coarse meat, without bone, and after boiling, or a quart of excellent broth, thickened with vegetables.

A prisoner is allowed to see his friends in presence of one of the officers, upon a representation from the chaplain, stating that he is entitled to the favour.

At his discharge he receives, in addition to the per centage, to which he is entitled, decent clothing, and suitable tools; and at the expiration of a year, if his conduct merits it, a further gratuity.

The duty of the chaplain is to read prayers and preach a sermon twice on a Sunday; to read prayers daily in the infirmaries; to obtain an intimate knowledge of the disposition and character of every prisoner; and to allot a considerable portion of his time to their religious instruction. He superintends their progress in reading and writing; and supplies them with suitable books and tracts. These various and important duties are, I have reason to think, faithfully performed.

Our first visit was to him: he gave us a very encouraging account of the effects of the system. He had observed visible amendment in many, and he thought that there was not one who had not received some degree of improvement. On the preceding (Christmas) day, he had admitted fifty to the Sacrament, all of whom he considered eligible; others he had refused.

His intercourse with the prisoners had led him to believe, that the general state of our jails, is a principal cause of the increase of crime. They had given him the most frightful descriptions of the scenes they had witnessed, and the language and practices to which they had been exposed; and he had come to the conclusion, from their representations, that if a person went into the generality of our prisons uncorrupted, it was next to impossible that he should go out so.

The governor fully confirmed the account given by the Chaplain, of the amendment of the Prisoners, and mentioned the observation of a man, who had lately been discharged: he said upon his release he had called at Newgate; and though he had been confined there four years, he never knew how bad it was till now, that he had experienced the difference between it and the Penitentiary.

The Governor told me, that "the grand secret was, *employment*. Labour was the right hand of police; that while the prisoners were employed, they were decent in their behaviour and language; but that if they were not engaged in work, they would be in mischief; that, in fact, he found, by repeated experience, that when work ended, his troubles began."

The women were all engaged in cooking, washing, ironing, and various kinds of needle-work; their earnings are about six pounds per annum; and their behaviour gave me a very favourable impression of the effects of employment, with religious instruction.

Those men who were at work, were shoe-makers, tailors, weavers, and one or two had learned to saw.

The surgeon sees every prisoner daily, and he made a very satisfactory report of their health, which was confirmed by their looks: he ascribes this to the regularity of their habits, and diet, their personal cleanliness, and the exclusion of intoxicating liquors.

Every part of the building was remarkably clean, and free from offensive smells.

Having thus endeavoured to do justice to the wisdom of the rules of this house of correction. I am induced, by the warm interest I take in its success, to point out some very lamentable deficiencies as to their execution; two-thirds of the men and the boys were totally unemployed, on December 26th. One boy, in six months' confinement, had learned a branch of trade, by which already he could earn six shillings per week. The next had learned nothing at all. And, at a late period, only one man in the whole prison had work.

I look upon the Penitentiary, at Millbank, as a grand national experiment of the effects of regular employment upon the depraved; but if employment is to be withheld, it becomes, in fact, an experiment of the effects of idleness. In one room in the second class, we observed some at work, and some without it. Amongst the latter, a boy of eleven years of age, whom we had long known. He has rendered himself remarkable by the extent of his depredations, and has been committed to various prisons, no less than eighteen times. To place him in idleness, in this assemblage of criminals, here to spend day after day, in receiving and imparting corruption, is, as to him, to give him no chance of reformation, and as to the system, is to defeat its very design, and to expect that corn will grow when you sow nothing but tares.

It is essential, that every person who comes there ignorant of a trade, should be taught one, and that he should be kept invariably to it. It is in vain to reply to this as has been replied,—" Men will not work except at the business they know: their pride is offended, at being put, as they call it, to school. Here, if any where, coercion is necessary. Their own welfare—the views of parliament—and the expectations of the country, must not be frustrated by such unsuitable haughtiness. They must be compelled to work, or the system must fail, and all the horrors and absurdities of the old method—commitments to hard labour, where nothing is to be done, and houses of correction, where all are corrupted—must be renewed, deriving authority and confirmation from the failure of this great and expensive attempt.

But I am far from thinking compulsion will be necessary. I asked a great many if they were willing to work, and invariably they lamented the hardship of having nothing to do, and expressed their willingness to do any thing. The Governor, in my presence, threatened one man to take away his work, and afterwards told me, the fulfilment of that threat would be the greatest punishment he could inflict.

At Ghent—at Philadelphia—at Bury—on the female side of Newgate—on the female side of this very Institution—all work, and consider it a privilege to be allowed to do so.

But it is contended that proper work is not procurable. At the "Refuge for the destitute," I saw many boys, and the average of their earnings, in making shoes, baskets, and clothes, was six shillings per week, at the end of the first year: twelve shillings at the end of the second: eighteen shillings at the end of the third. In the fifth they were capable of earning men's full wages. But I have a still stronger illustration. There never probably was a period in which labour was so difficult to be obtained, or so small in value as in 1817, and, perhaps, no part of England suffered so severely for want of work, as Spitalfields. From the extent of the distress, only the most helpless were admitted into the workhouse. Men were almost entirely excluded; and its inhabitants consisted principally of widows with large families, women near confinement, idiots, children, the sickly, the infirm, and the aged.

The average number of persons in this workhouse was 470:—viz.

Persons able to work	140
House servants, nurses who went out to attend the sick	40
Persons from age and infirmity, unable to work	200
Idiots and children	90
	470

	£.	s.	d.
The whole amount of earnings . . .	906	14	3
Allowance to the poor on their earnings, including the house servants . . .	218	4	0
Balance	£688	10	3

Considering that all these were more or less disabled, and that the benevolent managers of the poor had not the advantage of finding a market in the wants of government; this statement proves that all that is necessary to procure a provision of work at the Penitentiary, is ingenious contrivance, and vigilant attention to the demands for manufactured commodities.

Supposing, however, it should be found that while the decrepit are capable of productive labour in Spitalfields, the young and the vigorous are incapable at Millbank. Recourse must then be had to unproductive labour. It is a matter of no great concern to the state, whether a thousand pounds more or less is earned in this prison; but it is a matter of the utmost importance, whether the principle has, or has not, a fair trial.

Again then, I must entreat the managers of this institution, to direct all their energy to this point, and to consider the constant employment of every individual, as a measure of the most vital consequence. The failure, or success, of the scheme, the cause of humanity, so near to the hearts of its benevolent projectors, and so intimately connected with its successful issue, depend upon this; if these are released, who have served an apprenticeship to idleness, they will go forth, not reformed, but confirmed in those habits, which inevitably lead to crime. It would be sufficiently lamentable, to see our prisons again crowded with culprits, for whose improvement so much labour, time, and money, have been expended; but this is the least of the evils. The cause will suffer. This splendid establishment will stand a perpetual answer to every argument in favour of attempting reformation. Thus early then, I enter a protest against the efficacy of the Penitentiary system being decided by the result of this experiment, without it being fairly made. Without spending six hundred thousand pounds, the country might have known the effects of sloth; the question which justifies such an expenditure is, what are the effects of habitual industry?

I must here notice too, that one hour is too little for the prisoners to be in the open air, some out door work, something in the way of hard labour, ought to be provided, otherwise they will come out so tender, so sensible of the weather, as to be unfit for any but sedentary employments; the diet seems too ample for unemployed prisoners, but by a slight alteration, I think it might be made a stimulus to labour. The establishment now receives ninepence in every shilling, but it pays for meat, vegetables, potatoes, and porridge. Let it be ascertained what these cost, and let the amount be deducted from the share of the establishment, and credited to the prisoner. Let the establishment then furnish gratuitously nothing but one pound and a half of bread, except in particular cases; but give to the prisoner a power of applying this additional portion of his earnings, to the purchase of meat, &c. I am much deceived, if a man will not work more cheerfully and more industriously, if he finds the produce of his morning's labour in his dinner, and in his supper, than if he is to wait five years for it.

NOTE

To the Account of the Penitentiary, Millbank.

Since the publication of this pamphlet, I have received a communication from George Holford, Esq. M. P. which convinces me that some inaccuracies have crept into my description of the Penitentiary, at Millbank; the most material of which are—that the expenditure is over-rated; as, according to present estimates, it will fall short of 400,000*l.*; and the charge of future repairs in consequence of the nature of the soil, is also over-rated, as a method of effectually securing the foundations has been discovered: consequently, with the exception of the alterations already made—the two towers pulled down, and the two condemned—expense to any considerable extent is not to be apprehended. I must also add, that the conversation I have had with Mr. Holford has undeceived me with respect to the views of the Committee regarding labour. From what I saw, I feared that this vital requisite of all reformation in prisons, was not sufficiently estimated by them. All alarm of this sort is dissipated. I am now satisfied that no exertion will be wanting to introduce work, and that whatever deficiencies existed, when my observations were made, arose from the institution being as yet in its infancy—and the consequent impossibility of accomplishing at once, and in its earliest stage, those plans which are considered as essential to its future prosperity.

Had I been so fortunate as to converse with Mr. Holford prior to the publication, I should not have felt warranted in offering dvice, which I now see to be wholly needless: and I much regret that I should have said any thing which could give pain to Gentlemen, who, with no other motive than a desire to improve our prison discipline, having gratuitously devoted so large a portion of their time to the service of the public. Having fallen into mistakes, I do not hesitate a moment in retracting them; but, in my own justification, I must say, that the method I pursued of insuring correctness, seemed a very effectual one.—I derived my information almost exclusively from the Governor; I compared my memoranda with those of a gentleman of the highest respectability, who was my companion; and to prevent, as I thought, the possibility of error, in the presence of another gentleman of equally unquestionable character, I read over to the Governor each fact above stated. Confirmed by his acknowledgment of the truth of every particular, I sent the manuscript to the press the next day.

T. F. B.

March 16, 1818.

Proceedings of the Ladies' Committee, at Newgate.

About four years ago, Mrs. Fry was induced to visit Newgate, by the representations of its state, made by some persons of the Society of Friends.

She found the female side in a situation, which no language can describe. Nearly three hundred women, sent there for every gradation of crime, some untried, and some under sentence of death, were crowded together in the two wards and two cells, which are now appropriated to the untried, and which are found quite inadequate to contain even this diminished number, with any tolerable convenience. Here they saw their friends, and kept their multitudes of children, and they had no other place for cooking, washing, eating, and sleeping.

They slept on the floor at times one hundred and twenty in one ward, without so much as a mat for bedding, and many of them were very nearly naked. She saw them openly drinking spirits, and her ears were offended by the most terrible imprecations. Every thing was filthy to excess, and the smell was quite disgusting. Every one, even the Governor, was reluctant to go amongst them. He persuaded her to leave her watch in the office, telling her that his presence would not prevent its being torn from her. She saw enough to convince her that every thing bad was going on. In short, in giving me this account, she repeatedly said,—" all I tell thee is a faint picture of the reality; the filth, the closeness of the rooms, the ferocious manners and expressions of the women towards each other, and the abandoned wickedness, which every thing bespoke, are quite indescribable." One act, which I received from another quarter, marks the degree of wretchedness, to which they were reduced at that time. Two women were seen in the act of stripping a dead child, for the purpose of clothing a living one.

At that time she clothed many of the children, and some of the women, and read to them some passages in the Bible; and the willing and grateful manner, with which, even then, they attended to her admonitions, left upon her mind a strong desire to do more for their advantage, and a conviction that much might be done.

Circumstances, however, rendered any efforts, on her part, impossible, for the long period of three years.

About Christmas, 1816, she resumed her visits, and she found that many, and very essential, improvements had been made by the Jail Committee, especially, the females were less crowded, as they occupied, in addition to their former rooms, the state-apartments, consisting of six wards and three cells, and the yard attached to them; they were provided with mats, and two gratings were erected to prevent close communication between prisoners and their visitors: with all these improvements, however, the prison was a dreadful scene.

She found, she believes, all the women playing at cards, or reading improper books, or begging at the gratings, or fighting for the division of the money thus acquired, or engaged in the mysteries of fortune-telling: for then there was amongst them—one who could look into futurity, and the rest, who believed nothing else, were eager and implicit believers in the truth of her divinations.

Want of employment, was the subject of their continual lamentation. They complained that they were compelled to be idle, and that having nothing else to do, they were obliged to pass away the time in doing wrong. I cannot better describe their state than in the words of Mrs. Fry; "I soon found that nothing could be done, or was worth attempting for the reformation of the women, without constant employment; as it was, those who were idle were confirmed in idleness, and those who were disposed to be industrious, lost their good habits. In short, they went there to have the work of corruption completed, and subsequent examination has discovered to me the cases of many, who before this period had come to Newgate almost innocent, and who left it depraved and profligate in the last degree." As she had then no hopes of any provision of labour, her design was confined to about thirty children, whose miserable condition much affected her. They were almost naked, and seemed pining away for want of food, air, and exercise; but their personal sufferings was the least part of their wretchedness; what, but certain ruin must be the consequence of education in this scene of depravity? At her second visit she requested to be admitted alone, and was locked up with the women without any turnkey, for several hours; when she mentioned to those who had families, how grievous and deplorable she considered the situation of their offspring, and her desire to concur with them in establishing a school, the proposal was received, even by the most abandoned, with tears of joy. They said they knew too well the misery of sin, to wish to have their children brought up in it; that they were ready to do any thing which she might direct, for it was horrible, even to them, to hear their infants utter oaths and filthy expressions, amongst the first words they learned to articulate. She desired them maturely to consider the plan, for that she would not undertake it without their full and steady co-operation; but that if they were determined to persevere in doing their part, she would do hers, and that the first step would be to appoint a governess. This she left entirely to them, and they were to consider who was the most proper person for that appointment.

Consideration served only to confirm their desire for the instruction of their children. At her next visit they had selected a young woman as schoolmistress, and her conduct does credit to their discernment, for she has behaved throughout with signal propriety, and in no instance has she been known to transgress any rule. The elder women repeated their promises of entire obedience, if the trial might but be made; and several of the younger came to her, and entreated to be admitted to the intended school, saying, how thankful they should be for any chance of reformation.

Having thus obtained the consent of the females, her next object was to secure the concurrence of the Governor. She went to his house, and there met both the Sheriffs* and the ordinary. She told them her views, which they received with the most cordial approbation; but, at the same time, unreservedly confessed their apprehensions that her labours would be fruitless. At the next interview they stated, that they had thoroughly examined the prison, and were truly sorry to say they could not find any vacant spot suitable for her purpose, and therefore feared the design must be relinquished. Conclusive as this intelligence appeared, her heart was then too deeply engaged in the work, and her judgment too entirely convinced of its importance, to allow her to resign it, while one possibility of success remained. She again requested to be admitted alone amongst the women, that she might see for herself; and if her search then failed, she should be content to abandon her project. She soon discovered a cell which was unused, and this cell is the present school-room. Upon this she returned to the Sheriffs, who told her she might take it if she liked, and try the benevolent, but almost hopeless experiment.

The next day she commenced the school, in company with a young lady, who then visited a prison for the first time, and who since gave me a very interesting

* Messrs. Bridges and Kirby.

description of her feelings upon that occasion. The railing was crowded with half naked women, struggling together for the front situations with the most boisterous violence, and begging with the utmost vociferation. She felt as if she was going into a den of wild beasts, and she well recollects quite shuddering when the door closed upon her, and she was locked in, with such a herd of novel and desperate companions. This day, however, the school surpassed their utmost expectations: their only pain arose from the numerous and pressing applications made by young women, who longed to be taught and employed. The narrowness of the room rendered it impossible to yield to these requests, whilst a denial seemed a sentence of destruction, excluding every hope, and almost every possibility of reformation.

These ladies, with some others, continued labouring together for some time, and the school became their regular and daily occupation; but their visits brought them so acquainted with the dissipation and gross licentiousness, prevalent in the prison, arising, as they conceived, partly from want of certain regulations, but principally from want of work, that they could not but feel earnest and increasing solicitude to extend their institution, and to comprehend within its range, the tried prisoners. This desire was confirmed by the solicitations of the women themselves, who entreated that they might not be excluded. Their zeal for improvement, and their assurances of good behaviour, were powerful motives, and they tempted these ladies to project a school for the employment of the tried women, for teaching them to read, and to work.

When this intention was mentioned to the friends of these ladies, it appeared at first so visionary and unpromising, that it met with very slender encouragement: they were told that the certain consequence of introducing work, would be, that it would be stolen. That though such an experiment might be reasonable enough, if made in the country, among women who had been accustomed to hard labour; yet that it was quite destitute of hope, when tried upon those who had been so long habituated to vice and idleness. It was strongly represented that their materials were of the very worst description; that a regular London female thief, who had passed through every stage and every scene of guilt; who had spent her youth in prostitution, and her maturer age in theft and knavery; whose every friend and connexion are accomplices and criminal associates; is of all characters the most irreclaimable.

Novelty, indeed, might for a time engage their attention, and produce a transient observance of the rules of the school; but this novelty could not last for ever, the time would come when employment would be irksome, subordination would irritate their unruly feelings: deep rooted habits, modes of thinking and of acting imbibed in their cradles, and confirmed by the whole tenor of their lives, would resume their ascendancy. Violent passions would again burst out, and the first offence that was given, would annihilate the controul of their powerless and self-appointed mistresses. In short, it was predicted and by many too, whose wisdom and benevolence added weight to their opinions, that those who had set at defiance the law of the land, with all its terrors, would very speedily revolt from an authority which had nothing to enforce it, and nothing more to recommend it than its simplicity and gentleness. That these ladies were enabled to resist the cogency of these reasons, and to embark and to persevere in so forlorn and desperate an enterprize, in despite of many a warning without, and many an apprehension within, is not the least remarkable circumstance in their proceedings; but intercourse with the prisoners had inspired them with a confidence which was not easily to be shaken; and feeling that their design was intended for the good and the happiness of others, they trusted that it would receive the guidance and protection of Him, who often is pleased to accomplish the highest purposes by the most feeble instruments.

With these impressions, they had the boldness to declare, that if a committee could be found, who would share the labour, and a matron, who would engage never to leave the prison, day or night, they would undertake to try the experiment; that is, they would find employment for the women, procure the necessary money, till the city could be induced to relieve them from the expense, and be answerable for the safety of the property committed into the hands of the prisoners.

This committee immediately presented itself; it consisted of the wife of a clergyman, and eleven members of the Society of Friends. They professed their willingness to suspend every other engagement and avocation, to devote themselves to Newgate; and, in truth, they have performed their promise. With no interval of relaxation, and with but few intermissions from the call of other and more imperious duties, they have *lived* amongst the prisoners. At first, every day in the week, and every hour in the day, some of them were to be found at their post, joining in the employments, or engaged in the instruction of their pupils; and at this very period, when the necessity of such close attendance is much abated, the matron assures me, that, with only one short exception, she does not recollect the day on which some of the ladies have not visited the prison; that very often they have been with her by the time the prisoners were dressed; have spent the whole day with them, sharing her meals, or passing on without any; and have only left the school long after the close of day.

Having provided the committee, the next requisite was a matron. It so happened, that a gentleman who knew nothing of the objects in contemplation, called upon one of the committee, to ask her assistance in procuring a situation for a respectable elderly woman, whom he had long known. She was, in every way, competent to the office of matron, was willing to undertake it, and has discharged its duties with exemplary fidelity.

It became then necessary to apply to those in authority, by whose patronage and agency alone the design could be accomplished. Mr. Cotton, the ordinary, and Mr. Newman, the governor, were invited to meet Mrs. Fry at her husband's house. She represented to them fully her views, and the plans she proposed to adopt—the difficulties with which she saw herself surrounded; but with these, her sense of the importance of the object, and her confidence in superior direction. Mr. Cotton fairly told her, that this, like many other useful and benevolent designs for the improvement of Newgate, would inevitably fail. Mr. Newman bade her not to despair; but he has since confessed, that when he came to reflect upon the subject, and especially upon the character of the prisoners, he could not see even the possibility of success. Both, however, promised their warmest co-operation.

She next had an interview with Mr. Bridges, the sheriff; and having communicated to him her intentions, told him that they could not be carried into execution without the cordial support of himself and his colleague, or without the approbation of the City magistrates; from whom she asked nothing more at this time, than a salary for the matron, a comfortable room for her, and one for the committee. He expressed the most kind disposition to assist her, but told her that his concurrence, or that of the City, would avail her but little—the concurrence of the women themselves was indispensable; and that it was in vain to expect that such untamed and turbulent spirits would submit to the regulations of a woman, armed with no legal authority, and unable to inflict any punishment. She replied—"Let the experiment be tried; let the women be assembled in your presence, and if they will not consent to the strict observance of our rules, let the project be dropped. On the following Sunday, the two sheriffs, with Mr. Cotton and Mr. Newman, met the ladies at Newgate. Upwards of seventy women were collected together. One of the committee explained their views to them; she told them that the only practicable mode of accomplishing an object, so interesting to her and so important to them, was by the establishment of certain rules.

They were then asked, if they were willing to abide by the rules which it might be advisable to establish, and each gave the most positive assurances of her determination to obey them in all points. Having succeeded so far, the next business was to provide employment. It struck one of the ladies, that Botany Bay might be supplied with stockings, and indeed all articles of clothing, of their manufacture. She, therefore, called upon Messrs. Richard Dixon and Co. of Fenchurch-street, and candidly told them, that she was desirous of depriving them of this branch of their trade, and stating her views, begged their advice. They said at once, that they would not in any way obstruct such laudable designs, and that no further trouble need be taken to provide work, for they would engage to do it.

Nothing now remained but to prepare the room; and this difficulty was obviated, by the sheriffs sending their carpenters. The former laundry speedily underwent the necessary alterations—was cleaned and white-washed—and in a very few days the ladies' committee assembled in it, all the tried female prisoners. One of the ladies began, by telling them the comforts derived from industry and sobriety, the pleasure and the profit of doing right, and contrasted the happiness and the peace of those who are dedicated to a course of virtue and religion, with that experienced in their former life, and its present consequences; and describing their awful guilt in the sight of God, appealed to their own experience, whether its wages even here, were not utter misery and ruin. She then dwelt upon the motives which had brought the ladies into Newgate; they had left their homes and their families, to mingle amongst those from whom all others fled; animated by an ardent and affectionate desire to rescue their fellow-creatures from evil, and to impart to them that knowledge, which themselves, from their education and circumstances, had been so happy as to receive.

She then told them, that the ladies did not come with any absolute and authoritative pretensions; that it was not intended that they should command, and the prisoners obey; but that it was to be understood, that all were to act in concert; that not a rule should be made, or a monitor appointed, without their full and unanimous concurrence. That for this purpose, each of the rules should be read, and put to the vote; and she invited those who might feel any disinclination to any particular, freely to state their opinion. The following were then read:—

RULES.

1. That a matron be appointed for the general superintendence of the women.

2. That the women be engaged in needle-work, knitting, or any other suitable employment.

3. That there be no begging, swearing, gaming, card-playing, quarrelling, or immoral conversation.—That all novels, plays, and other improper books, be excluded; and that all bad words be avoided: and any default in these particulars be reported to the matron.

4. That there be a yard-keeper chosen from among the women; to inform them when their friends come; to see that they leave their work with a monitor when they go to the grating, and that they do not spend any time there, except with their friends. If any woman be found disobedient in these respects, the yard-keeper is to report the case to the matron.

5. That the women be divided into classes, of not more than twelve; and that a monitor be appointed to each class.

6. That monitors be chosen from among the most orderly of the women that can read, to superintend the work and conduct, of the others.

7. That the monitors not only overlook the women in their own classes, but if they observe any others disobeying the rules, that they inform the monitor of the class to which such persons may belong, who is immediately to report to the matron, and the deviations to be set down on a slate.

8. That any monitor breaking the rules shall be dismissed from her office, and the most suitable in the class selected to take her place.

9. That the monitors be particularly careful to see that the women come with clean hands and face to their work, and that they are quiet during their employment.

10. That at the ringing of the bell, at 9 o'clock in the morning, the women collect in the work-room, to hear a portion of scripture read by one of the visitors or the matron; and that the monitors afterwards conduct the classes from thence to their respective wards in an orderly manner.

11. That the women be again collected for the reading, at six o'clock in the evening, when the work shall be given in charge to the matron by the monitors.

12. That the matron keep an exact account of the work done by the women, and of their conduct.

And as each was proposed, every hand was held up in testimony of their approbation.

In the same manner, and with the same formalities, each of the monitors was proposed, and all were unanimously approved.

When this business was concluded, one of the visitors read aloud the 15th chapter of St. Luke,—the parable of the barren fig-tree, seeming applicable to the state of the audience. After a period of silence, according to the custom of the Society of Friends, the monitors, with their classes, withdrew to their respective wards in the most orderly manner.

During the first month, the ladies were anxious that the attempt should be secret, that it might meet with no interruption; at the end of that time, as the experiment had been tried, and had exceeded even their expectations, it was deemed expedient to apply to the Corporation of London. It was considered, that the school would be more permanent, if it were made a part of the prison system of the city, than if it merely depended on individuals. In consequence, a short letter, descriptive of the progress already made, was written to the Sheriffs. The next day an answer was received, proposing a meeting with the ladies at Newgate.

In compliance with this appointment, the Lord Mayor, the Sheriffs, and several of the Aldermen attended. The prisoners were assembled together, and it being requested that no alteration in their usual practice might take place, one of the ladies read a chapter in the Bible, and then the females proceeded to their various avocations. Their attention during the time of reading; their orderly and sober deportment, their decent dress, the absence of every thing like tumult, noise, or contention, the obedience, and the respect shewn by them, and the cheerfulness visible in their countenances and manners, conspired to excite the astonishment and admiration of their visitors.

Many of these knew Newgate, had visited it a few months before, and had not forgotten the painful impressions made by a scene, exhibiting, perhaps, the very utmost limits of misery and guilt. They now saw, what, without exaggeration, may be called a transformation. Riot, licentiousness, and filth, exchanged for order, sobriety, and comparative neatness in the chamber, the apparel, and the persons of the prisoners. They saw no more an assemblage of abandoned and shameless creatures, half naked and half drunk, rather demanding, than requesting charity. The prison no more resounded with obscenity, and imprecations, and licentious songs; and, to use the coarse, but the just, expression of one who knew the prison well, "this hell upon earth," exhibited the appearance of an industrious manufactory, or a well regulated family.

The magistrates, to evince their sense of the importance of the alterations which had been effected, immediately adopted the whole plan as a part of a system of Newgate, empowered the ladies to punish the refractory by short confinement, undertook part of the expense of the matron, and loaded the ladies with thanks and benedictions.

About six months after the establishment of the school for the children, and the manufactory for the tried side, the committee received a most urgent petition from the untried, entreating that the same might be done amongst them, and promising strict obedience. In consequence, the ladies made the same arrangements, proposed the same rules, and admitted in the same manner, as on the other side, the prisoners to participate in their enaction. The experiment has here answered, but not to the same extent. They have had difficulty in procuring a sufficiency of work, the prisoners are not so disposed to labour, flattering themselves with the prospect of speedy release; besides, they are necessarily engaged, in some degree, in preparations for their trial. The result of the observations of the ladies has been, that where the prisoners, from whatever cause, did no work, they derived little, if any, moral advantage; where they did some work, they received some benefit; and where they were fully engaged, they were really and essentially improved.

A year is now elapsed since the operation in Newgate began, and those most competent to judge, the late Lord Mayor and the present, the late Sheriffs and the present, the late Governor and the present, various Grand Juries, the Chairman of the Police Committee, the Ordinary, and the officers of the prison, have all declared their satisfaction, mixed with astonishment, at the alteration which has taken place in the conduct of the females.

It is true, and the Ladies' Committee are anxious that it should not be concealed, that some of the rules have been occasionally broken. Spirits, they fear, have more than once been introduced; and it was discovered at one period, when many of the Ladies were absent, that card playing had been resumed. But, though truth compels them to acknowledge these deviations, they have been of a very limited extent. I could find but one lady who had heard an oath, and there had not been above half a dozen instances of intoxication, and the Ladies feel justified in stating, that the rules have generally been observed. They have been treated with uniform respect and gratitude. They have reason to rejoice in the improved conduct, and, as they trust, in the confirmed moral habits of the prisoners. Several have received the rudiments of education and have learned, for the first time, the truths of the Christian religion. Many have left them, who are now filling their stations in life uprightly and respectably. But one discharged from the prison, has been again committed for a transgression of the law.

In the infirmary I saw a woman, who was represented as near her end. She spoke very feelingly of the Ladies, adding, "all the comforts around me, and all the consolation of my mind, are owing to them."

With respect to gaming, I must mention an anecdote, which displays the efficacy of the system pursued. A session had just closed, many of the former prisoners were sent away, and many new ones were received. A report was circulated that gaming was still practised in the prison: one of the Ladies went there alone, and assembled the prisoners together, she told them what she had heard, and that she feared it was true; she dwelt upon the sin of gaming, its evil effect upon their minds, the interruption it gave, and the distate it excited, to labour; and she concluded by telling them, how much the belief of that report had grieved her, and how gratified she should be, if, either from consideration for themselves, or kindness to her, they should be disposed to relinquish the practice. Soon after she retired to the Ladies' room, one of the prisoners came to her, expressed, in a manner which indicated real feeling, her sorrow for having broken the rules of so kind a friend, and gave her a pack of cards; and four others did the same. Having burnt the cards in their presence, she felt bound to remunerate them for their value, and to mark her sense of their ready obedience by some small present. A few days afterwards she called the first to her, and telling her intention, produced a neat muslin handkerchief. To her surprise, the girl looked disappointed; and, on asking the reason, she confessed that she had hoped that Mrs. ——— would have given her a Bible, with her own name written in it, which she should value beyond any thing else, and always keep and read. Such a request, made in such a manner, could not be refused; and the Lady assures me, that she never gave a Bible in her life, which was received with so much interest and satisfaction, or one, which she thinks more likely to do good. It is remarkable, that this girl, from her conduct in her preceding prison, and in court, came to Newgate with the worst of characters; she has read her Bible with tolerable regularity, and has evinced much propriety of conduct, and great hopes are entertained of her permanent improvement.

In addition to the encouragement received by the Ladies, from the conduct of their pupils, both within and without the prison, they have the satisfaction of hearing other and important testimonies. The Governor, the Matron, and the Chaplain of the Penitentiary at Millbank, assured me, that the females, who came from Newgate, were far more correct and decent, than those who were sent from any other prison. The manner in which these asked after the welfare and health of the Ladies' Committee, was highly interesting. I can truly say, I never heard more minute or more affectionate inquiries, or more grateful acknowledgements. The answer of one struck me much, but more from the manner than the language. Mentioning the name of one of the Ladies, I asked, if she had done them any good. The reply was, "God bless her, and the day she came to Newgate: she has done us all good, and we have, and shall always have, reason to bless her."

This prisoner had been in Newgate previously, as well as subsequently, to the introduction of the Ladies' Committee, and gave me a striking picture of the contrast between the two periods. At the first, the filth and smell were so intolerable, as immediately to affect her health. There was no employment but gaming, drinking, obscene song-books and conversation. Her friends, who happened to be respectable, were entirely excluded; they dared not enter the prison. Her mother had, indeed, made the attempt, but her shawl had been openly snatched from her, and she could not recover it. Men, generally thieves, connected with the women, were admitted without any restraint, and very often slept there; but when the Ladies came, all this was altered, and the women soon seemed as much changed in mind, as they were in their practices.

The effect wrought by the advice and admonitions of the Ladies, may, perhaps, be evinced more forcibly by a single and a slight occurrence, than by any description. It was a practice of immemorial usage, for convicts, on the night preceding their departure for Botany Bay, to pull down and to break every thing breakable within their part of the prison, and to go off shouting, with the most hardened effrontery. When the period approached for a late clearance, every one connected with the prison, dreaded this night of disturbance and devastation. To the surprise of the oldest turnkey, no noise was heard, not a window was intentionally broken. They took an affectionate leave of their companions, and expressed the utmost gratitude to their benefactors; the next day they entered their conveyances without any tumult; and their departure, in the tears that were shed, and the mournful decorum that was observed, resembled a funeral procession; and so orderly was their behaviour, that it was deemed unnecessary to send more than half the usual escort.

If any thing further could be wanting to establish the success of the institution, I could appeal to the manufactory. The women have made upwards of twenty thousand articles of dress, not one of which has been lost or stolen.

Thus has an experiment been tried, as important (in the contemplation of its future results) as any that was ever attempted by ingenious humanity. In one sense it is much to be lamented, that the scene of action was not more favourable. The narrow limits of Newgate, and the consequent impossibility of classification, prevented the adoption of many measures, which might have contributed much to the improvement of the prison; and might, therefore, have rendered the result more strikingly successful. On the other hand, we must rejoice that the trial has been made under every possible disadvantage. A system which has surmounted the peculiar and numerous obstacles which Newgate presented, must prevail where the means of separation are greater, and the turpitude of the prisoners is less. Here, if any where, failure was to be expected.

It is evident that there is a great difference in the heinousness of crimes. There is too, as great a difference in the character of persons guilty of the same crime. A country girl may commit an offence, but her mind probably will not have received the deep taint of habitual depravity, and a sense of shame, if not of remorse, will not have entirely fled. An inhabitant of London (such at least as those on whom this experiment was tried) may be guilty of precisely the same offence, but this is but one act of a series of similar acts, one exemplification of a regular system.

Newgate at the period described, contained, and

indeed at all periods must contain, the refuse of the capital; that is, the very worst description of criminals, committed for the very worst excesses of crime. Women who had been frequent inmates of prison, and with whom thieving was their "daily bread;" with such unpropitious materials, success is conclusive, as to the possibility of reformation elsewhere.

It will naturally be asked, how and by what vital principles, was the reformation in Newgate accomplished? how were a few Ladies, of no extraordinary influence, unknown even by name to the magistrates of the metropolis, enabled with such facility to guide those who had baffled all authority, and defied all the menaces of the law,—how was it that they

> "Wielded at will this fierce democracy?"

How did they divest habit of its influence? By what charm did they transform vice into virtue, riot into order? When I first heard of their proceedings, when I heard that Mr. Newman the Governor had declared, that after the lapse of a fortnight he hardly knew again this part of the prison, so entire was the change; I confess that the foregoing questions occurred to my mind:—a visit to Newgate explained them. I found that the Ladies ruled by the law of kindness, written in their hearts, and displayed in their actions.

They spoke to the prisoners with affection, mixed with prudence. These had long been rejected by all reputable society. It was long since they had heard the voice of real compassion, or seen the example of real virtue. They had steeled their minds against the terrors of punishment, but they were melted at the warning voice of those who felt for their sorrows, while they gently reproved their misdeeds: and that virtue which discovered itself in such amiable exertions for them, recommended itself to their imitation with double attractions.

With so much experience as the Ladies committee have had, it is a matter of importance to ascertain what plans they can recommend, as having been found of principal efficacy. These are:—

1st, "Religious instruction,"—perusal of the Scriptures morning and evening. They have found the prisoners remarkably ignorant of the first principles of Christianity, and they have reason to think that a prison, in excluding many objects of worldly interest, occupation, and pleasure, and in the pause which it produces in the career of life, and in the apprehensions it sometimes excites, is well calculated for the inculcation of religious impressions.

2dly, Constant employment is a grand and an indispensable requisite in the reformation of a prison. They would feel themselves totally incompetent to restrain the passions of this unruly race, if their minds were not engaged in useful and active objects.

3dly, Rules simple and lenient, but rigidly enforced, and if possible, the concurrence of the prisoners in their formation.

4thly, Classification and separation, to the greatest possible extent.

5thly, They recommend that prisoners should be treated as human beings, with human feelings; with that disinterested kindness which will engage their affections; yet as human beings degraded by crime, with that degree of restraint, and with those symbols of degradation, which may recall a sense of their guilt, and humble their pride.

I am well aware that I have dwelt longer upon this subject than its connexion with the object of the book may justify; but if it be a digression, I trust my readers will excuse it, in consideration of its importance and interest. Were it merely a philosophical experiment, it would be worthy of authentic record, as giving us an insight into the secret structure of the human mind; as furnishing a demonstration that there is rarely a period at which the embers of expiring virtue may not be revived: but it is not an abstract metaphysical discovery, it is intimately connected with the welfare and happiness of mankind, and with the diminution of crime. Thousands pass through our prisons every year, and learn there, vice and the arts of successful villany. A judicious application of the methods adopted by these ladies, may furnish the prisoners with other acquisitions, and render our prisons what they ought to be, and what they are not, schools of morality and reformation.

Conclusion.

Having thus described two distinct and opposite modes of prison discipline, I would suggest to my reader, that a comparison of these is the most certain criterion of their respective merits.

That vice and misery are produced by the one, and prevented by the other, may be gathered from the following facts:—

On the 14th December, 1817, an account was taken at my request of the number of prisoners in the second station in Newgate, who had been there before. It appeared that out of two hundred and three, forty-seven of those convicted, besides seven of those acquitted, had within the two preceding years, been confined there. It is probable that many (passing under fictitious names, and anxious to appear as offenders for the first time, which might operate in mitigation of their sentence), were not recognized. Newgate, it is to be remembered, is but one prison among several; many who had never been there before, were known to have been in the other jails of the metropolis and county. Amongst the boys, of the ten first I examined, five confessed that they had previously been convicted of other crimes. Taking these circumstances into consideration, we may fairly presume that forty per cent. of those discharged from prison return there again, and this calculation is considerably lower than that made by all the jailers of London and its vicinity, whom I have consulted.

In the jails at Bury, Philadelphia, and Ghent, five per cent. is the average return.

In *Newgate*, the number of prisoners from May 16th, 1817, to January 1, 1818, was 1500.

Of these, 511 were admitted to the infirmary as seriously ill, besides several who were excluded from want of accommodation, and many whose indisposition was too slight to require confinement. Of the latter description, there were daily about eighteen cases. Upon these data, we may fairly compute, that considerably above one third of the prisoners suffer more or less from disease.

At *Bury*, amongst 128 prisoners, not one was unwell.

At *Ghent*, amongst 1300, twenty-five only were ill.

At *Philadelphia*, not having as yet received an account of the exact numbers, I can only state that their health is remarkably good; recalling to the recollection of my reader this important fact, that with the alteration of the system, a reduction took place in the charges of the physician, to the extent of three fourths.

Of the two systems thus compared, it is, I imagine, evident that the one is *unjust*: to the convicted delinquent, because it imposes upon him rigours to which he is not sentenced;—to the unconvicted, because it inflicts upon him a very serious punishment before trial.

Is *illegal*, as it transgresses the letter of many statutes; and still more strongly, as it violates all the equitable principles, and the very spirit of the British Constitution.

Is *partial*, as it annexes to the same crime very different degrees of punishment, and the same punishment to very different degrees of crime. The rules of one county, appointing in its jails, cleanliness, labour, sufficiency of diet, attention to health, moral and religious instruction, and classification. The rules of the next county, approving filth, sloth, insufficiency of food, carelessness of health, and instruction in nothing but the arts of iniquity; and these without any discrimination between prisoners, whether tried or untried, whether for trivial offences or for atrocious crimes.

Is *cruel*, as appears by the condition in which the prisoners are often found.

Is *impolitic*, as it frustrates the two great ends of punishment, the prevention of crime, and the reformation of the criminal; as it raises up, educates, and matures offenders.

Is *extravagant*, as these offenders live upon the public, being supported in prison by the funds of the country and out of it, by the spoliation of private property.

Is *unworthy of a great and wealthy kingdom*, as it corrupts national morality, and disgraces national character.

In short, its direct and inevitable tendency is, to produce misery and vice.

It is also evident that the other system is merciful and wise; while it consults the health and suitable accommodation of the prisoner, it strikes at the roots of his criminality, his ignorance, idleness, and debauchery; while it corrects his habits, it subdues his temper. By friendly admonitions and religious instruction, it awakens a consciousness of his former depravity, and of its present and eternal consequences. It shews to him the value of a fair and reputable character, and encourages him in its pursuit, by proving that it is attainable even by him: it makes reformation possible. Thus by giving a sense of religion, habits of industry and temperance, its tendency is to prevent misery and vice.

If my reader goes with me the length of these conclusions, I trust he will concur with me in another; that a change of system ought immediately to be made. Not a mere alteration of a few regulations in a few districts, but such a change as shall comprehend every prison, (not yet amended) in the United Kingdom.

So great a work can only be accomplished by the legislature, but the legislature will feel with the people; and if public attention be once aroused to the subject, the day of reformation will not be very distant, and Great Britain may become in this, as she is in so many other branches of political wisdom, an example to the surrounding nations; instead of being (as was observed by a foreign gentleman well acquainted with the subject, as he went round Newgate), an instructive warning of principles to be rejected, and practices to be avoided, in the management of prisons.

In the advancement of this design, every individual of any influence will find a department for himself. The service which may be rendered to the cause by members of parliament and magistrates is evident; but the formation of societies for procuring intelligence, their communication with that which already exists in London, diligent and accurate investigation of prisons, and the publication of these, must have a very powerful effect. I am well persuaded that the evil exists only because it is unknown; that it arises not from insensibility on the part of the nation, but from ignorance; and that a faithful disclosure of the scenes which may be witnessed in almost every county jail, would speedily be followed by an impulse to prevent them.

A conviction of these truths, as it has been my motive for this publication, so it is my only apology for its length.

FINIS.

For EU product safety concerns, contact us at Calle de José Abascal, 56–1°,
28003 Madrid, Spain or eugpsr@cambridge.org.

www.ingramcontent.com/pod-product-compliance
Ingram Content Group UK Ltd.
Pitfield, Milton Keynes, MK11 3LW, UK
UKHW012339130625
459647UK00009B/403

* 9 7 8 1 1 0 8 0 0 4 9 2 3 *